A Biblical Theology of Missions

by

Paul York

Table of Contents

List of Figures

The Africa's Hope Discovery Series

This book is part of the *Discovery Series* developed by Africa's Hope. We believe that this series will become an important tool for training church leaders in Africa. Our goals for the Discovery Series reflect our purpose.

> Our mission is to facilitate training
> > that equips the church in Africa
> > > to disciple all nations
> > > > in the power of the Holy Spirit.

To *facilitate training*, the Discovery Series texts are designed to support study in classrooms and small groups. As the name of the series implies, this series helps the learner "discover" knowledge. You will see six features in the texts that promote active learning.

- Unit pages divide the book into its major parts and summarize the chapters.
- Comments in "Sidebars" highlight key phrases and encourage application.
- Graphs, charts, and illustrations reinforce key concepts.
- Review and discussion questions end every chapter.
- A glossary defines key terms.
- Study Questions for each chapter are listed at the end of the text.

To better *equip the church in Africa*, this series was written with the African minister in mind. This commitment is reflected in the choice of words, in the illustrations, and the applications to African issues. The specific target audience for these texts is:

- diploma-level study for Bible school students.
- pastors who have completed a similar level of pastoral training.
- laymen and laywomen who sense a call into some form of ministry.

We believe that it is Africa's time to disciple all nations. The revival among the Pentecostals in Africa is one of the most significant revivals in church history. We hope these texts are foundational to a training process that will enable thousands of Africans to proclaim Christ to the nations. For this reason, this text and others will emphasize that the role of the African Church is world mission.

Ministry in the power of the Holy Spirit is another recurring theme in the Discovery Series. We believe that knowledge should never be separated from the anointing of the Holy Spirit. The Discovery Series writers and editors are committed to balancing good scholarship and practical application. The goal is to produce men and women of God who are capable of ministering effectively in the African pastoral context.

The Course Description

This course, *The Biblical Theology of Missions*, is an introductory study of the mission of God as it is found throughout the Bible — the *Missio Dei*. It explores the biblical theology of the mission of God. It also shows the implications of this theology for people called by God to pastor, evangelize, disciple, teach, and cross cultural barriers with the gospel.

Author's Note

My father, Dr. John V. York, was widely known in Assemblies of God World Missions as a teacher, preacher, mentor, and educator who focused on the Mission of God (Missio Dei). My father's life message was that the singular mission of God found in Scripture is the advance of the gospel to all nations of the earth in the power of the Holy Spirit. It was my father's conviction (and is mine as well) that the amazing opportunity of partnering with God in His mission is the privilege and purpose statement of every born again Christian — regardless of continent, race, gender, or language.

It is my inestimable privilege to enter into my father's work and ministry burden in the writing of this new text. Dr. York completed his B.A. level textbook, *Missions in the Age of the Spirit*, in 2000, but never put into print his heart for the mission of God for the broadest audience in Africa — the entry level pastoral and missionary training schools and colleges of the continent.

This book is a work done in honor and memory of my father's love for Africa and for the mission of God; but it is also a book done with my own family and church and my own students at Central Bible College in mind. The foundational thoughts are my father's; any errors or weaknesses discovered are only my own.

My father's last words to me, spoken a few days before his homegoing in December 2005, were the following: "Missio Dei...the Gospel!.. All Nations... everywhere. That's it!" It is in the spirit of Dr. John York's own deep conviction about God's mission, and its daily relevance to the very core of all Christian life and ministry, that I dedicate this work. May the King of the nations and Lord of the harvest raise up the greatest generation of kingdom workers yet seen in this, the eleventh hour of God's great harvest!

The Author and Developmental Team

The author of *The Biblical Theology of Missions*, Paul York, currently serves as the Chairman of the Missions and Evangelism Division at Central Bible College, Springfield, Missouri, U.S.A. Reverend York was raised in Nigeria with his missionary family. His higher educational formation began at Northwest College of the Assemblies of God, Kirkland, Washington where he earned a B.A. degree (1990). In 1994, he earned an M.A. degree in Missiology from the Assemblies of God Theological Seminary, Springfield, Missouri, U.S.A.

Before coming to Central Bible College, Reverend York and his wife Lisa served as Assemblies of God missionaries in Ethiopia. Later, the Yorks served as nationally appointed *Chi Alpha* Campus Missionaries in Texas, U.S.A. Reverend York also served as missionary in residence at Southwestern Assemblies of God University, Waxahachie, Texas. The Yorks are the parents of a son, John, and a daughter, Lauren.

A development team operates under the direction of Africa's Hope curriculum committee. Members of this team include Dr. Carl Gibbs, Dr. Denis Tyson, and Dr. David Duncan. Others involved in checking the appropriateness of course content for the target audience include Dr. Edgar Lee and Dr. Denzil Miller.

Unit 1
The Foundation of the Missio Dei

Chapter 1   –   Biblical theology shows God's mission in our world; theme of all Scripture is the mission of God; God introduced as Creator of the world; all God's people can know Him and represent Him; all people, though sinners, valuable to God and His servants; shame, separation, and death result from sin; and God's plan to redeem lost humanity

Chapter 2   –   Seeds of hope given as God judges sin; ungodly mankind judged at Flood, but godly Noah and family rescued; God's judgement at Babel: the confusion of languages; God's mercy prepared for new language groups

Chapter 3   –   Abraham's call and God's relationship with him; the Abrahamic Covenant and its promise: "All nations will be blessed through you"; what God's promise reveals about His plans for lost humanity; fallen mankind won't be destroyed; God's intent to redeem fallen people and bless them; God's promise the organizing theme for Scripture and the purpose for the church today

CHAPTER 1

Creation and the Fall of Man

Introducing the Mission of God

Christians learn about God through reading the Bible and through their own experiences with Him. They learn that the God of the Bible is an active God. He is not absent, distant, quiet, or distracted. Instead, God is present in our world. He is near to us. He is speaking to us. He is making His glory known to people in all the earth. God is on a mission!

Mankind's Rebellion and God's Mercy

God first acted to create our world, and He gave all of us life. However, mankind chose to rebel against God. We disobeyed His clear commands. We wandered into sin and self-destruction (Genesis 3:6).

At this point God could have withdrawn from humanity. He could have even destroyed us all and started creation over again. Instead, God has acted a second time. This time He acted to bring salvation to humanity:

> *The Lord looked and was displeased that there was no justice.*
> *He saw that there was no one,*
> *He was appalled that there was no one to intervene;*
> *So His own arm worked salvation for him…*
> *From the west men will fear the name of the Lord,*
> *And from the rising of the sun, they will revere His glory*
> *(Isaiah 59:15b-16, 19a).*

The actions God has taken are powerful to change humanity. God does not simply encourage us to stop sinning and do good deeds. Instead, He actually "redeems" or buys people back from the destructive control of sin. People who are redeemed by God become His new creation. They are able to display God's glory to all the earth.

God's mighty acts are in agreement with His divine plan. He brings salvation to guilty sinners and changes them into a new people. They then display His glory in all the earth.

God's plan is to advance His kingdom throughout the world through the preaching of the gospel. This is His "mission." A mission is a coordinated set of activities that are used to reach a specific goal. God's goal is to display His glory throughout the Earth by transforming disobedient sinners into His own dear children. His mission is the worldwide spread of the wonderful gospel message:

> *…God was reconciling the world to Himself in Christ,*
> *not counting men's sins against them.*
> *And He has committed to us the message of reconciliation.*
> *We are therefore Christ's ambassadors,*
> *as though God were making His appeal through us.*
> *We implore you on Christ's behalf: Be reconciled to God*
> *(2 Corinthians 5:19-20).*

It is clear that God has committed Himself to a plan of action for the world. Instead of destroying mankind for rebellion, He is offering to save the world. He wants to restore man's lost friendship with Himself. He is announcing a program of reconciliation for unsaved humanity! This program is sometimes called the *Missio Dei* or the mission of God.

This course will introduce you to the mission of God. Once you know God's mission, you will be better able to understand God's plan for the church. You will also begin to see a divine purpose for your own life. God is on a mission, and He is sharing that mission with us!

God is on a mission, and He is sharing that mission with us!

Understanding the Bible

In this book you will study many verses found throughout the *Bible* that show the mission of God. It is recommended that you mark these verses in your own study copy of the Bible with a pen or pencil as you are reading this textbook. When you begin to mark verses that show the theme of Scripture, you will see the pages of your Bible "come alive" with reminders of God's great purposes in the world. These are also God's purposes for your church and for your own life!

You may want to mark texts that advance the *Missio Dei,* using an underscore or a special color or symbol in the margin. This will help you to use these texts in your future ministry. May you enjoy these lessons and teach them to others as long as you serve God in His work.

The Mission of God and the Church

The Bible is the written Word of God to mankind that reveals to us the will and character of God. It also tells the story of God's intervention with mankind. In other words, the Bible reveals God's mission to us. By reading the Bible, we can discover what God is doing in the Earth and how He is doing it.

The Bible tells us the story of God's mission in the past. It also shows us the future when God's mission will be gloriously completed — when all nations will worship God in heaven!

In between the past and the future is a period of time in which God's mission is being put into action on Earth. This is the time in which we live. God has created a church to communicate His glory to all peoples on Earth.

Unfortunately, those in the church are not always aware of God's great plan to redeem people from every nation. Believers today sometimes become distracted with the problems or temptations of this life. They may become discouraged or wonder if there is any true purpose for their lives.

God's Ministers Must Know His Mission

The wise minister will always seek to better understand God's mission. Such a minister will avoid distractions by looking to the big picture of what God is doing in His divine mission. Then the wise servant of Christ will live his or her life in line with God's great plan, and will help God's church to do the same. This strategy will yield two great results.

First, the minister that focuses on the mission of God will ensure that his or her life's work is not in vain. How can a life lived in line with God's purposes be wasted? God will take the sincere efforts of a person who is living for His mission and grant wonderful success to his or her work. If a minister has joined hands in partnership with God, God's strength will ensure the result.

Second, the minister that focuses on the mission of God will never lack for purpose and meaning in his or her life. He or she will always feel a joy and dignity that comes only from doing God's work along with Him. We are God's chosen people, and we are doing God's work! Remember: God is on a mission and He is sharing that mission with us.

Using the Bible to Learn about God's Mission

It is a marvelous thing to have God's written Word available to us. One of the reasons the Bible is so valuable is that is shows us God's mission. In fact, the Bible is organized around the theme of the mission of God.

Scholars of theology use the Latin term *missio Dei* (mission of God) to describe the theme of the Bible. The term *missio Dei* is widely used in the Assemblies of God fellowship in Africa and around the world because it represents God's whole redemptive plan for the world in one simple phrase. This course will use the Bible to teach you about the *Missio Dei*.

Many people read the Bible without seeing any real connection to its books. However, each book of the Bible was inspired by the one true God. The human writers who wrote down the Scripture did so under the inspiration of God's Holy Spirit. This means that the Bible's sixty-six books not only share a common author (the Holy Spirit) but also a common theme (the *Missio Dei*).

The Bible contains history, poetry, prophecies, gospels, and letters. When you look at the Bible as a whole, you realize that it is actually one great Story — the story of God's love for a fallen and sinful humanity and what God has done to win us back to Himself. In fact, the theme of the entire Bible is the mission of God!

Let us take a journey through the Bible. It will be a journey across time, starting at the earliest moments of creation and continue through the days of the Bible. The story is still going on today, and your life is a part of it!

The theme of the entire Bible is the mission of God!

Because this study is a Biblical Theology, you will be asked to read many verses. You will need a Bible nearby to look up many of the references. Other important verses will be printed in the center of the page. By the time you reach the end of the Bible, you will see glimpses into events still to come. God is going to bring His story to a glorious conclusion.

> *The kingdom of the world*
> *has become the kingdom of our Lord*
> *and of His Christ,*
> *and He will reign for ever…*
> *(Revelation 11:15).*

From time to time this text will ask you to take time for prayer about the things you have been studying. If you are in a study group, read this prayer and then take time to seek God together. As you pray, the words of Scripture will be marked on your hearts and minds in a new way. Let us pray together before we begin our exploration of the *Missio Dei* throughout Scripture!

Prayer #1

"Almighty Father,
we thank You for loving us enough to intervene in our world.
If You had not saved us, we would have lived a miserable life,
destined for destruction in hell.
Instead, we have become beloved children of God.
We are citizens of a heavenly kingdom that will last forever.
Show us how to live as citizens of Your kingdom!
Show us how to behave as children of the Father!
Reveal to us Your purposes.
Help us to see the Missio Dei in Your wonderful Book.
Open our minds to understand,
soften our hearts to respond,
and transform our wills to obey.
We pray in Jesus' powerful name —
Amen!"

Figure 1.1

The mission of God is the proclamation of the gospel in the power of the Spirit to all nations of the world (York, 19). Read the following verses to learn more about the *Missio Dei*.

Concerning Scripture
- *2 Timothy 3:16*

Concerning God's plan for the entire world
- *Genesis 12:3*
- *Matthew 24:14*
- *Matthew 28:18-20*

The Creator of the World

A wise man has said that a good place to start is in the beginning. The first five books of the Bible are grouped together. The great majority of the verses in all five books were written by Moses, the servant of the Lord. When these five books are discussed as a group, they are called the "Pentateuch." The Pentateuch begins with the first verse of the book of Genesis: "In the beginning God created the heavens and the earth" (Genesis 1:1).

The first thing God shows us is that He (God) existed at the beginning. God already existed when time began. In the beginning — God!

The Nature and Work of God

God is not a man. He has no birthday. He has no father or mother. In theological terms, God is "pre-existent" (He was there before time began) and "eternal" (He lives beyond time, unconfined by a beginning or an end).

How great our God is! He is not burdened to prove His existence to us; He simply announces His presence in Genesis 1:1. God does not have to prove that He exists because He is the eternal Creator. The farmer does not have to prove to his harvest that he exists; instead, the harvest exists in response to the work of the farmer. If anyone must prove his or her existence, it is we the creation — not the One who made us!

After showing us the existence of God, this verse reveals the fact that God created the heavens and the earth. Take time now to read aloud the following verses. They show us that God created a good world out of nothing, simply by the power of His word.

Read Genesis 1:3, 6-7, 9, and 14-15. The God we serve is indeed the Creator of the Universe. He is to be worshipped and obeyed!

Now read Genesis 1:11, 20-21, and 24. Here we see that the God who created the world is also the Giver of the gift of life. These opening words in the Bible teach us to respect life because it is the gift of God. Nothing lives without His permission. God's works are to be valued by mankind.

The Value of God's Creation

Today we live in a world with many problems. Perhaps we have forgotten that God created a wonderful world for us to enjoy. The world God made was not spoiled by rebellion and sin: "God saw all that he had made, and it was very good" (Genesis 1:31).

God alone is responsible for the existence of creation. God has a purpose for all that He has made. All that God made was very good!

These truths contrast with the teachings of many other religions. They often describe an accidental or incomplete creation. Christianity teaches that God is the eternal Creator, and everything He made is complete and good.

The rest of the Bible speaks of God again and again as the Creator. As the good Creator of all, God has the right to rule over all places and all people in the world. Every people group should submit to the rule of the Creator. Those who cooperate with God's rule belong to God's "kingdom of light." Those who refuse to do so are described as followers of another kingdom, the "dominion of darkness."

> *The Father…has qualified you*
> *to share in the inheritance of the saints in the kingdom of light.*
> *For he has rescued us from the dominion of darkness*
> *and brought us into the kingdom of the Son he loves…*
> *(Colossians 1:12-13).*

The rest of creation is assigned its place to glorify God, but mankind must choose which kingdom to live in: either the kingdom of rebellion and darkness, or the kingdom of God and the light.

The Image of God

After showing us God's creation of the world and His gift of life, the Bible then reveals to us the greatest act of the Creator:

> *Then God said, "Let us make man in our image…"*
> *So God created man in his own image,*
> *in the image of God he created him;*
> *male and female he created them*
> *(Genesis 1:26-27).*

Genesis clearly emphasizes that the man was not like the rest of the creation. Both the male and female were made in the image of God. They were like God in some special way. They were different from all other created things.

Implications of Being Made in the Image of God

What does it mean that we are made in the image of God? This is one of the great foundational truths of Scripture. There are two great lessons to learn.

First, those made in the image of God are capable of knowing Him. Unlike the earth or heavens or animals, humans can hear God speak and can communicate with Him. We are uniquely valuable because we alone of all earthly creation can have a relationship with God!

Second, those made in the image of God are capable of representing Him. Those who can hear God speak are also capable of telling others what God is saying. They can be God's messengers or agents. God can give people a job to do. When God selects a man or woman to serve Him, that person is capable of agreeing. He or she can willingly obey what God desires.

> *Anyone made in the image of God is capable of knowing and representing God!*

The very way man was made showed the close connection and concern of God for mankind. Rather than simply speaking the word, God forms the man from the dust and breathes life into him. (Read Genesis 2:7 to discover the unique way that God gave life to the first man.)

Imagine how valuable people are to God. They alone, out of all the created world, are made in the Image of God! They could know God, and they could make God known to one another. These wonderful abilities are the glory that God has given to people. We must respect one another because of the value God has invested in us.

God Gives the Man a Job — and a Partner

After making the man as a special creation, God immediately gave him a job. Adam was God's representative in the naming of the animals. Genesis describes God and Adam in close communication. Adam was busy doing important work in God's creation on God's behalf. The work Adam did gave him a sense of value and dignity.

> *Now the Lord God had formed out of the ground*
> *all the beasts of the field and all the birds of the air.*
> *He brought them to the man to see what he would name them;*
> *and whatever the man called each living creature, that was its name.*
> *So the man gave names to all the livestock,*
> *the birds of the air and all the beasts of the field*
> *(Genesis 2:19-20).*

Naming the animals was not a small, unimportant job. In science, this task is known as "taxonomy." God trusted Adam to represent Him well by naming and classifying the animals in His wonderful creation!

God is not distant from His new creation. Instead, God is concerned about Adam's life. He noticed that even in the perfect Garden of Eden, Adam had a problem. There was no other person for Adam with whom to share life. God did not want the man to live his life alone.

> The Lord God said, "It is not good for the man to be alone.
> I will make a helper suitable for him"
> (Genesis 2:18).

Adam enjoyed all the animals that God had let him name. However, Adam still felt a loneliness for someone of his own kind; therefore, God decided to create a suitable partner for Adam!

It is important to emphasize that both men and women are made in God's image. The man was made first. The woman was made second, not to be ruled over by the man, but to be his unique partner. She was not his servant or slave; instead, she was a "suitable helper" for his life.

> But for Adam no suitable helper was found.
> So the Lord God caused the man to fall into a deep sleep;
> and while he was sleeping, he took one of the man's ribs
> and closed up the place with flesh.
> Then the Lord God made a woman from the rib he had taken out of the man,
> and he brought her to the man
> (Genesis 2:20b-22).

This text shows us how precious the woman was. She was unique in all of God's creation. Adam's words concerning the woman were words that show her importance. He gave her a name as well, and he was united with her as her husband. You can read about it in Genesis 2:23-24.

Lessons from the Creation of Mankind

What can be learned from the account of the creation of mankind? It is important to remember that all people are made in the image of God. Men, women, and children alike can know God and can represent Him. They are valuable because they are made in the image of their Creator — not because of their family background or race or language or sex.

We are called to minister in a world that values some people more than others. One child may be valued by his or her parents while another child is rejected. Some people rejoice when sons are born but act sorrowful at the birth of daughters. Some people prefer their own ethnic group and show hatred or indifference to others. God disagrees with these human values.

What a powerful message we have as Christians! It is good news for men, women, and children alike. We are able to tell any individuals we meet that they are valuable to God. All people should be important to us as well because we serve their Creator. From the very beginning, the Bible makes it clear that all people are important to God.

A Christian must not forget this and slip into a non-Christian way of thinking. We represent God in this world; so we must live by His message. God sees each person as valuable because each person is capable of knowing and representing Him.

Summary

God is not distant from people; He is closely involved with all peoples. God's "mission" is His divine plan to advance His kingdom throughout the world through the preaching of the gospel. A mission is a coordinated set of activities that are used to reach a specific goal. The Bible's sixty-six books share a common author (the Holy Spirit) and also a common theme (the *Missio Dei*). One may read the Bible as a story and find that the *Missio Dei* advances clearly across time.

Review and Application

———————◆———————

Now that you have completed the study of this chapter, you should ask these questions: "What do the truths I have just studied mean in my situation?" Or, "How can I apply these principles in my work as a pastor and leader?"

1. What is a "mission?"

2. Give the definition of the "mission of God."

3. Give two reasons why wise ministers will organize their study and ministries around the theme the "mission of God."

4. Explain how the Bible can be studied across time to discover the *Missio Dei.*

5. How could you use the following Scriptures to explain the mission of God to a new believer: 2 Timothy 3:16, Genesis 12:3, Matthew 24:14, and Matthew 28:18-20?

6. Explain the two great lessons we learn from the fact that humans are created "in the image of God."

Be prepared to discuss these questions and any questions or issues that come to mind when your instructor refers to them in class.

Judgments and Promises

*A*fter creation, Scripture prepares the way for God's mission to be announced. People rebel against God, and in this they become deserving of God's holy judgment. However, after each obstacle to God's plan, God replies with a promise. Instead of destroying them, He promises that He will indeed reach out to save lost people.

Mankind's Fall into Sin

God had created an entire garden for the first couple to live in and take care of for Him. He had left one tree from which Adam and Eve were not to eat. This was done to give them a chance to obey God willingly.

Our free choice to serve God is important. God wants us to serve Him willingly, not because we are forced to do so. Satan wanted to attack God, and he decided to do it by tempting the free will of God's human creation.

Where did Satan and his evil come from? God does not think it important to explain this to us in Genesis. We know that Satan also was created, because only God is eternal. However, everything that God creates is good. Satan may have been the first created being to use free will to rebel against God. Having fallen himself, Satan now introduces temptation and evil to humanity.

> *Now the serpent…said to the woman,*
> *"Did God really say, 'You must not eat from any tree in the garden'?"*
> *(Genesis 3:1).*

Satan came to the woman and tempted her to doubt the truthfulness, love, and wisdom of God. Adam and Eve had no reason to doubt any of these things, and they had every reason to obey their Creator and friend. However, they chose to consider and accept the temptation.

Satan brought the occasion to sin. However, Adam and Eve both knowingly chose to disobey their Creator. Read about this sad event in Genesis 3:6.

The Results of Sin

The results of sin began immediately. Sinning did not improve their situation as Satan had promised Eve. Like the first couple, we also are tempted to sin in order to gain some supposed advantage. However, sin never leads to any real improvement. Instead, it brings heartbreaking problems into our lives.

For the first time in their lives, Adam and Eve felt shame. They felt separated from God and from each other. All they could do was try to cover their shame; however, their efforts were not satisfactory.

> *Then the eyes of both of them were opened,*
> *and they realized they were naked;*
> *so they sewed fig leaves together and made coverings for themselves*
> *(Genesis 3:7).*

Our efforts to cover our sins are always inadequate. Fig leaves could not cover their shame. Today people try to cover their sin with fine clothing, possessions, wealth, fame, rebellion, or pleasure. Yet none of these things can take away our sin before God.

Imagine a world without any guilt or shame! Such a world is almost impossible for us to understand, but this is where the first couple had been living. Now Adam and Eve's own sin had destroyed the ideal environment created by God.

Since they had damaged God's perfect creation, Adam and Eve now tried to hide from God when He came near.

> *Then the man and his wife heard the sound of the Lord God*
> *as He was walking in the garden in the cool of the day,*
> *and they hid from the Lord God among the trees of the garden.*
> *But the Lord God called to the man, "Where are you?"*
> *(Genesis 3:7-9).*

Did God know where Adam and Eve were hiding? Indeed, God knows everything. He knew exactly where Adam and Eve were, and He also knew what they had done. However, He was giving the first couple a chance to confess their sin and repent.

God could have destroyed them as sinners in that moment; however, they were valuable to Him. They were made in His image, capable of knowing and representing Him; so God chose to give them a chance to repent.

When God spoke the words, "Where are you?" He was asking a question that we must still answer today. To God's question, we should reply "Here I am, trapped in my own sin, guilty and helpless. Can you save me even now?" The wonderful truth is that God will save the one who repents!

"Here I am, trapped in sin. Can you save me even now?"

God had to punish Adam and Eve's sin; so He placed a curse on the man, the woman, and the serpent in order to punish their sins. Yet in the middle of the curse we find words that also showed He was not willing to destroy mankind.

This teaches us an important lesson: God's punishment is always intended to help someone. God does not judge in order to destroy sinners

God's judgments are always redemptive in nature.

in His anger. Instead, God's judgments are redemptive in nature. This means that His judgments have power to draw people back into relationship with Him.

The judgment of God may convince the person who is punished to confess. If the person will not confess, God's judgment may make such an example of that person that other people who hear of it may repent of their sins before it is too late.

A Seed of Hope in the First Judgment

God does not judge out of violent anger nor does He punish people without reason. God's punishments in general are given to redeem someone. This is true of the first judgment scene in the Bible in Genesis 3.

> *So the Lord God said to the serpent,*
> *"Because you have done this,*
> *'Cursed are you above all livestock and all the wild animals!*
> *...I will put enmity between you and the woman,*
> *and between your offspring and hers;*
> **he will crush your head,**
> **and you will strike his heel'"**
> *(Genesis 3:14a, 15; emphasis mine).*

God's promise in Genesis 3:15 came after the first disaster, the fall of man. Mankind was now separated from God by sin. Guilt and shame would be a barrier between man and God. Sin would make life difficult and the tempter would try to destroy all people.

However, God would also give the woman a special descendant or offspring who would one day crush the head of the serpent! In Hebrew, the word "offspring" is the word "seed." A seed of hope was given even during the first judgment. The hope was this: one day Satan would be defeated by a man God would send to save the world!

This promise is often called the "first Gospel." The details of the plan were not yet clear. Still, this plan of God was wonderful news for Adam and Eve. God was promising to intervene in human history to save fallen humanity.

The Second Judgment

The Pentateuch revealed to us the foundations of God's mission to bless all nations. After Creation, the Fall, and the appearance of nations, God began to work with the family of Abraham. He gave Abraham one of the most crucial or central promises in the entire Bible: ". . . and all peoples on earth will be blessed through you" (Genesis 12:3). He then confirmed this central promise with a binding covenant. Abraham's children would become a nation of their own, a kingdom of priests with a mandate to bless the whole world.

Now it is time to follow the progress of God's great story throughout the rest of Scripture. God will send new promises that make His earlier promise more clear. What will happen next as God moves to bless the nations and overcome the evil of sin that was chosen by mankind?

The story of God's mission to save mankind, even though He must judge man's sin, continues with the accounts of the Flood and the Tower of Babel. These accounts give us the story behind the existence of nations.

In the flood, we see that God was grieved by the great sinfulness of mankind. It is very significant to realize that God is affected by the results of human sin. God is never guilty of sin, but our sin causes Him pain!

> *The Lord saw how great man's wickedness on the earth had become,*
> *and that every inclination of the thoughts of his heart*
> *was only evil all the time.*
> *The Lord was grieved that He had made man on the earth,*
> *and His heart was filled with pain*
> *(Genesis 6:5-6).*

God sent a great flood to punish people's sin. God could have destroyed all people in the flood because of their sins. He could have stopped the pain caused by the rebellion of the people that He loved. Instead, He chose to show them grace. He did this by saving Noah, a man who respected and lived for God.

God's Covenant with Noah

The flood destroyed all life except for the people and animals in the Ark; however, God rescued Noah and gave mankind a fresh start. For the second time in Genesis we see that after a great disaster, God gave a promise:

> *Then God said to Noah and to his sons with him:*
> *"I now establish my covenant with you...*
> *Never again will all life be cut off by the waters of a flood;*
> *Never again will there be a flood to destroy the earth...*
> *This is the sign of the covenant I am making between me and you...*
> *I have set my rainbow in the clouds,*
> *and it will be a sign of the covenant"*
> *(Genesis 9:8-9a, 12-13).*

This promise was something new. A covenant was given. A covenant is a promise agreement in which two parties willingly agree to certain requirements in order to form a lasting relationship.

For instance, a marriage is a covenant in which a man and a woman promise to love and care for one another in an exclusive relationship. The sign of a marriage covenant in some societies is a ring. The ring serves to remind everyone of the covenant promises made by the one who wears it.

Covenants help to ensure the future of a relationship. God was still seeking a relationship with mankind in spite of the great pain man's sin had caused Him. He gives a sign of the new covenant. He gives this sign not because He may forget His promise someday but because mankind may forget God.

In fact, even with the sign of God's covenant, Noah's descendents soon forgot God. This is always the tendency of the human heart. The apostle Paul wrote about this problem:

> *For although they knew God,*
> *they neither glorified Him as God nor gave thanks to Him,*
> *but their thinking became futile*
> *and their foolish hearts were darkened…*
> *they became fools*
> *and exchanged the glory of the immortal God for images…*
> *Furthermore, since they did not think it worthwhile*
> *to retain the knowledge of God,*
> *He gave them over to a depraved mind, to do what ought not to be done*
> *(Romans 1:21, 22b-23, 28).*

Mankind knew God, but did not think it worthwhile to retain that knowledge! Oh, how great our sinfulness and folly is. Yet in spite of this, God still desires a relationship with us. We do not deserve any grace, but He has shown very great grace to us. Let us take a moment to pray to the Lord.

Prayer #2

Almighty Father,
We see from Your Word how much we have forgotten.
Although our fathers once knew God,
they threw that knowledge away.
Sin has entered each of our hearts, and we have welcomed it there.
Now we see wickedness all around us, just as in the days of Noah
before the flood.
Lord, we repent for the wicked forgetfulness of humanity!
Please forgive us of our own sin and rebellion.
Now that You have saved us and offered us a chance
to know God again,
also give us grace to do better than our early fathers did before us.
May we retain the knowledge of God
and never forget to maintain a relationship with You!
Amen.

Figure 2.1

Noah's descendents soon fell into the forgetfulness that the apostle Paul was discussing. Instead of obeying God's command to spread out over the earth (Genesis 9:1), they decided to stay together and form one great city. At the center of the city was a monument to human rebellion and pride — the Tower of Babel.

> *Now the whole world had one language and a common speech.*
> *As men moved eastward, they found a plain in Shinar and settled there.*
> *They said to each other, "Come, let's make bricks and bake them*
> *thoroughly"...*
> *Then they said, "Come, let us build ourselves a tower that reaches to the*
> *heavens,*
> *so that we may make a name for ourselves*
> *and not be scattered over the face of the whole earth."*
> *But the Lord came down to see the city and the tower that the men were*
> *building*
> *(Genesis 11:1-3a, 4-5).*

All of Noah's descendents spoke one language since they were from the same family. They moved eastward to Shinar or Babylonia which in modern days is in southern Iraq. Here they mastered new technologies for building, and they decided to build a man-centered rather than a God-centered society.

Their new city would focus on their own abilities and desires. Instead of spreading across the earth as God had directed, they chose to stay together. Instead of worshipping God in God's way, they would create their own tower to heaven. This tower was a religious symbol. They would replace the one true God with human religion.

God had seen before what happens when the people were allowed to go on sinning together, and He moved to judge the people of the city. Remember: God's ultimate intention for punishment is the redemption of people!

> *The Lord said,*
> *"If as one people speaking the same language*
> *they have begun to do this,*
> *then nothing they plan to do will be impossible for them.*
> *Come, let us go down and confuse their language*
> *so they will not understand each other."*
> *So the Lord scattered them from there over all the earth,*
> *and they stopped building the city.*
> *That is why it was called Babel* [confused] —
> *because there the Lord confused the language of the whole world*
> *(Genesis 11:6-9a).*

God knew that people united in wickedness would be successful in forgetting God; so He divided the peoples by doing something brilliant and completely new — He changed their languages!

This is one of the most amazing miracles in the Bible, because language is one of the deepest parts of the human identity. Language is one of the things that separates us from the animals and displays the image of God in us. In fact, the science of language (linguistics) suggests that the language we learn is responsible in part for teaching us how to think.

The confusion of the languages at Babel required God to change the minds and memories of the people at a level deeper than their conscious daily thought life. God is all powerful, and He was able to change the languages in the minds and hearts of the people in a moment. Truly God is mighty!

The resulting confusion was called "Babel." Different groups of people could no longer communicate and get along; so they began to drift apart from each other. God's judgment caused the people to fulfill His plan of repopulating the whole earth. God's judgment also increased the possibilities that someone would decide to serve Him. If one group rejected God, perhaps another would be more open to His message.

Genesis chapter 10 came after Genesis 11 in time. Chapter 10 is often called "The Table of Nations." Look back at this chapter in your Bible, including verses 1 and 32. In this list or table, you will see that God was concerned with the existence and lifestyles of many peoples.

The account of Babel is very important to our understanding of the mission of God. The languages we deal with today are not accidental barriers. Neither can they be ignored. They are an example of one of God's redemptive judgments. They were created to restrain human wickedness until humanity could be redeemed.

Once people of one language begin to be redeemed, they must begin to be concerned with the languages of other unsaved people around the world. All of the unsaved peoples are important to God, for He lists each one of the first seventy peoples by name in Genesis 10. If God cares about all the languages and people groups on earth, so must we.

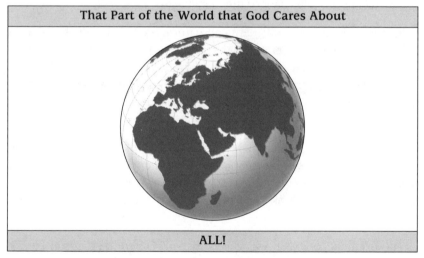

That Part of the World that God Cares About

ALL!

Figure 2.2

If sinners united in their sinning can succeed at forgetting about God, how much more will believers united in God's mission be able to succeed at making Christ known throughout all the earth!

Summary

Since all people are created in God's image, God's mission is to give all people the chance to become His loyal followers. In addition, God's mission will include people made in His image who become His messengers. The doctrine of the image of God helps us answer questions such as "Who will be the people that God loves?" and "Who will God use to bring those people into His kingdom?" People became liable to judgment due to their choice to sin. However, God gives hope that He will act to redeem all people, even though He must judge their sins.

Review and Application

Now that you have completed your study of chapter 2, you should ask questions such as these: "What do the truths about the mission of God I've studied in this chapter mean to me?' And, "How may I apply the principles I've studied in my preaching and teaching ministry?"

1. Sin often looks attractive to us, but it is very disappointing. What are some of the results of sin?

2. Did God know where Adam and Eve were hiding? If He did, then why did He ask the question, "Where are you?"

3. God called out "Where are you?" when Adam and Eve were hiding. How is God still asking sinners this question today? How do people reply?

4. What is a covenant?

5. If all people are descended from both Adam and Noah, they must once have spoken the same language. Where then did the many languages of the earth today get their beginnings?

Be ready to discuss these questions and any other questions or issues that come to mind when your instructor refers to them in class.

CHAPTER 3

A Nation to Bless All Nations

*T*he Bible moves quickly from the time of Noah to the time of Abraham, although many years passed. God was doing a new thing. He chose a single man and made a covenant with him that would endure throughout time. This man's children would become a nation chosen to bless all the other nations of the world!

The "Fiery Center" of the Word of God

Take special note to mark the verses that follow in your Bible. The promise found here becomes the organizing theme for the rest of Scripture. It has been called "the fiery center" of the Word of God!

> *The Lord had said to Abram,*
> *"Leave your country, your people and your father's household*
> *and go to the land I will show you.*
> *"I will make you into a great nation*
> *and I will bless you; I will make your name great*
> *and you will be a blessing.*
> *I will bless those who bless you, and whoever curses you I will curse;*
> *and **all peoples on earth will be blessed through you"***
> *(Genesis 12:1-3; emphasis mine).*

God did not choose the man Abraham as a way to exclude the other peoples of the world but rather as a way to include them. The peoples of the world were far from God; so God chose to create a new covenant relationship with a single man, Abram, and his descendents. However, the covenant blessings God gave to Abram made it clear that he and his children existed to bring God's blessings to all peoples on the earth.

There are six promises in the list of God's covenant blessings for Abram. The last promise is the greatest. In the place of the ungodly nation of Babel, God promises to form the children of Abram into a godly nation.

Abram will be blessed by God — better than that, he will have the joy of becoming a blessing! God will make Abram's name great. He will also bless those who bless Abram, and curse those who curse him.

Greatest of all is the grand promise at the end of the list. Through Abram, all peoples on earth will be blessed (York, 25)!

The Blessing Is for All

It is the amazing word "all" that captures our attention here. God's plan was not just to bless the Jews. God does not favor certain people groups over others. He intends in the end that all nations will be blessed!

The first 11 chapters of Genesis serve as an introduction to the rest of the Bible. At the end of these chapters several things are clear. Creation is the work of God, and all that God has made is good. All people are made in God's image.

However, mankind has fallen into sin. People are responsible for their sins. God could do away with people, but instead He chooses to redeem them. The nations and languages matter to God. Finally, we see that God will act to bless every nation on earth through the family of one man — Abraham.

God's plan is in place. The rest of the Bible will develop across time to show the way that God chose to bring blessing to all peoples. We are included in His list! Also included are many kinds of people who do not yet serve the Lord at all.

God is still in the process of fulfilling this one great promise to Abraham. Our lives have a part in the fulfillment of it.

God is on a mission, and He is sharing part of that mission with us!

The Covenant with Abraham

Genesis continues to tell the story of the children of Abram. Although Abram did not fully understand it yet, God planned to make his family into a new nation that would experience the blessed life in God's kingdom. This new nation would serve as a sign to other nations. It would cause other nations to desire to know the one true God.

God now develops His promise by establishing a covenant with Abram. The name Abram means "exalted father." God later renamed him Abraham or "father of many nations" (Genesis 17). From this point, we shall refer to him by his more familiar name Abraham.

Remember: a covenant is a promise agreement in which two parties willingly agree to a list of requirements in order to form a lasting relationship. Genesis 15 tells us in more detail about the establishment of God's covenant with Abraham.

The Doubts of the Man of Faith

Abraham is known as the Father of Faith; however, the occasion of this covenant was not Abraham's great faith, but his doubts:

> *But Abram said, "O Sovereign Lord,*
> *what can you give me since I remain childless*
> *and the one who will inherit my estate is Eliezer of Damascus?"*
> *And Abram said, "You have given me no children…"*
> *Then the word of the Lord came to him: "This man will not be your heir,*
> *but a son coming from your own body will be your heir."*
> *He took him outside and said,*
> *"Look up at the heavens and count the stars — if indeed you can count them."*
> *Then He said to him, "So shall your offspring be."*
> *Abram believed the Lord, and He credited it to him as righteousness*
> *(Genesis 15:2-3a, 4-6).*

Abraham was worried, for he knew God had promised to multiply his family and make it a blessing to all peoples on earth. However, he was old and still he had no children! In fact, Abraham's wife Sarah was past the age of bearing children, and he owned no land. If his promised children were ever born, they would have no base from which to operate in their task of blessing all the earth. So he presented his case to God.

In spite of the passing of time, God answered that His plan was still in place. Abram's children would become more numerous than the stars!

Imagine Abram standing outside of his tent, looking at the stars that appeared in the night sky. Perhaps he counted as many as he could. To think that he would be the father of a people as numerous as the stars!

Abraham chose to believe God; so God counted his trusting faith as righteousness (Genesis 15:6). We also may be counted as righteous if we continue to believe in God's promises. He has chosen to use ordinary people to evangelize and disciple people in your country and around the world. We can believe in His ability to use us, too.

God "Cuts a Covenant" with Abraham

Next, God told Abraham that He would give him the land in which his children would be based:

> But Abram said, "O Sovereign Lord,
> how can I know that I will gain possession of it?"
> So the Lord said to him, "Bring me a heifer, a goat and a ram,
> each three years old, along with a dove and a young pigeon."
> Abram brought all these to him, cut them in two
> and arranged the halves opposite each other....
>
> As the sun was setting, Abram fell into a deep sleep,
> and a thick and dreadful darkness came over him...
> When the sun had set and darkness had fallen,
> a smoking firepot with a blazing torch appeared
> and passed between the pieces.
> On that day the Lord made a covenant with Abram
> and said, "To your descendents I give this land...."
> (Genesis 15:8-10a, 12, 17-18a).

What was God doing in this sacrifice? He was "cutting a covenant" with Abram. This was the accepted way of establishing the promises of a covenant agreement at that time. It was an interesting process in which a time for sacrifice would be arranged. The leaders of the two groups making the new covenant would cut the animals in half and arrange them on either side of a ceremonial walkway. Then they would walk where the blood flowed between the pieces of the animals.

In this way, they were saying: "If I fail to fulfill the covenant promises I am making today, make my life like the lives of these animals. My life is lost if I do not fulfill these solemn promises!"

God arranged for the cutting of a covenant with Abram; however, God did not require Abram to walk between the pieces. God alone did this, perhaps so that Abram would not lose his life if he failed to obey. God appeared in a visible, fiery form and passed between the pieces.

God was saying, "If I fail to fulfill my promises to you, Abram, my life is lost! If I fail to give you a land and heirs — and through them, make your descendents a blessing to all nations on earth — then I will cease to exist!"

Abraham believed in God's promises and obeyed God's covenant. We in the church should also believe in God's mission and obey the requirements of His new covenant with us.

New Testament References to Abraham's Covenant

In the New Testament there are many references to Abraham and the promise that he would bless all nations. We see this clearly in the book of Galatians:

> *The Scripture foresaw that God would justify the Gentiles by faith,*
> *and announced the Gospel in advance to Abraham:*
> *'All nations will be blessed through you.'*
> *So those who have faith are blessed along with Abraham,*
> *the man of faith"*
> *(Galatians 3:8).*

Another great reference to Abraham's covenant is found in the book of Hebrews. This passage explains the reason for the encouragement we have in our faith. It refers to the establishment of the *Missio Dei* covenant with Abram.

> **When God made His promise to Abraham,**
> *since there was no one greater for him to swear by, he swore by himself,*
> *saying, "I will surely bless you and give you many descendents."*
> *And so after waiting patiently, Abraham received what was promised.*
> *Men swear by someone greater than themselves,*
> *and the oath confirms what is said*
> *and puts an end to all argument...*
> **God wanted to make the unchanging nature of his purpose very clear**
> *to the heirs of what was promised,*
> *he confirmed it with an oath.*
> *God did this so that,*
> *by two unchangeable things in which it is impossible for God to lie,*
> *we who have fled to take hold of the hope offered to us*
> *may be greatly encouraged.*
> **We have this hope as an anchor for the soul, firm and secure.**
> *(Hebrews 6:13-19a; emphasis mine).*

Hebrews says that God's covenant oath to Abraham gives us a hope that is still an anchor for our souls today. What an important promise this is!

Why did God swear this oath to Abraham? It was not necessary from God's point of view, for God had already made up His mind to use Abraham's family to bless all nations.

This oath was only necessary as an act of kindness to assist the faith of God's people. God spoke to them in a way that they could understand so that they would choose to obey Him. God did not swear the oath of the covenant with Abraham to make His intentions more certain to Himself. Instead, God swore the oath of the covenant to make Abraham more certain of His intentions.

Did God Keep the Covenant?

Did God keep His covenant oath? The ongoing account of the people of Israel answers this question. Over four hundred years after Abraham died, God made his descendents into a large group of people who became the new nation of Israel.

Israel was about to enter the land God had promised them. This was the first opportunity for foreign nations to observe Israel, the new people of God.

The wicked King Balak hired Balaam, a false prophet, to curse Israel when Israel was about to enter their promised land. However, when Balaam tried to "see" a false vision of destruction for Israel, God helped him to "see" something different. Balaam, while trying to curse Israel, said this instead:

> *God is not a man, that he should lie,*
> *nor a son of man, that he should change his mind.*
> *Does he speak and then not act? Does he promise and not fulfill?*
> *I have received a command to bless;*
> *he has blessed, and I cannot change it…*
> *The Lord their God is with them;*
> *the shout of the King is among them…*
> *There is no sorcery against Jacob, no divination against Israel.*
> *It will now be said of Jacob and of Israel, 'See what God has done!'*
> *(Numbers 23:19-20, 21b, 23).*

Here, at the first opportunity for other nations to inspect God's people, God's covenant blessings are already being clearly seen by those foreign nations.

The account of the covenant with Abraham is the story of how God gave us the gift of faith. The legacy Abraham leaves us is the gift of enduring faith in God's announced mission. God is truthful: What He promises, He will fulfill. All peoples will indeed be blessed through the descendents of Abraham. May God's name be praised!

The Kingdom of Priests

God did indeed give Abraham a son whose name was Isaac (Genesis 21:1-5). Isaac in turn had a son named Jacob, and Jacob's twelve sons eventually moved to Egypt. The children of Abraham lived there for 400 years.

Although He waited for many years, God never forgot His promises to Abraham. He blessed the family until it grew into a great nation of people, the Israelites (Exodus 1:6-7). However, the Egyptians put Israel into slavery. Eventually God raised up a man named Moses to be a deliverer of His people Israel. The story is told in the book of Exodus.

The name "Exodus" means "the road out." In this book God takes a very large number of Abraham's descendents and leads them out of Egypt toward the land He had promised them. In addition, God was leading His people on a journey out of spiritual confusion and into a new covenant relationship with Himself.

God sent Moses to speak to the people. In doing this, God was revealing Himself to Israel, and He was also giving them a new identity.

> *Therefore say to the Israelites:*
> *"I am the Lord,*
> *and I will bring you out from under the yoke of the Egyptians.*
> *I will free you from being slaves to them,*
> *and I will redeem you with an outstretched arm*
> *and with mighty acts of judgment.*
> *I will take you as my own people,*
> *and I will be your God.*
> *Then you will know that I am the Lord your God,*
> *who brought you out from under the yoke of the Egyptians.*
> *And I will bring you to the land I swore with uplifted hand*
> *to give to Abraham, to Isaac and to Jacob...*
> *I am the Lord"*
> *(Exodus 6:6-8).*

The process of forming Israel into God's special people was long and difficult. Just like their fathers before them, the Israelites were people with doubts and sins that held them back. God was merciful and He determined to use them anyway. They were the beginning of the great family of children God had promised to Abraham. They had a special job to do in God's plan for mankind.

In order to teach the Israelites about their place in His plan, God miraculously brought the people out of Egypt (Exodus 7-14) and led them to Mount Sinai. Here in the desert, far from all distractions, God spoke to His people.

> *In the third month after the Israelites left Egypt — on the very day —*
> *they came to the Desert of Sinai...and Israel camped there*
> *in the desert in front of the mountain.*
> *Then Moses went up to God,*
> *and the Lord called to him from the mountain and said,*
> *"This is what you are to say to the house of Jacob*
> *and what you are to tell the people of Israel:*
> *'You yourselves have seen what I did to Egypt,*
> *and how I carried you on eagles' wings*
> *and brought you to myself.*
>
> *Now if you obey me fully and keep my covenant,*
> *then out of all nations you will be my treasured possession.*
> **Although the whole earth is mine,**
> **you will be for me a kingdom of priests**
> *and a holy nation.'*
> *These are the words you are to speak to the Israelites"*
> *(Exodus 19:1, 2b-6; emphasis mine).*

Just as a potter might form a lump of clay into a useful shape, so God was shaping the multitude of Abraham's children into a useful nation. They were no longer a group of abused slaves; they had been miraculously delivered from Egypt by the Almighty God!

With the Israelites' new freedom came new responsibility. God was calling them to obey His covenant fully. If they obeyed, they would be God's treasured possession.

God is clear to emphasize that He is not only the God of the Israelites, for "the whole earth is mine" (Exodus 19:5b). However, out of all peoples on earth, Israel would be chosen to be "a kingdom of priests" (Exodus 19:6).

What does this mean? A priest is someone who stands between men and God. A priest's ministry involves two kinds of speaking: speaking to the people for God (preaching and teaching), and speaking to God for the people (prayers and petitions). Being a priest also involves holiness which means separation. Someone who is holy is separated *from* the ways of others and separated *to* the purposes of God.

We know from the books that follow that Israel had a tribe of ministers, the Levites, and from the Levites the descendents of Aaron who served as priests. The Levites were to be holy servants who taught the Israelites God's truth. They also assisted the priests with the people's spiritual needs.

However, the ministry of the Levitical priesthood is not the fulfillment of God's promise in Exodus 19:6. The promise was not that the new kingdom would *have* priests; rather, the promise was that the whole new kingdom would *be* priests!

> *"'Although the whole earth is mine,*
> *you will be for me a kingdom of priests*
> *and a holy nation.'*
> *These are the words you are to speak to the Israelites."*
> *(Exodus 19:5b-6)*

Remember: in the ministry of any priest three parties must be involved: God is on one side, people are on the other, and the priest is in the middle. The priest's ministry is to connect God and the people in covenant relationship.

The nation of Israel was to serve as priests for all the other nations.

In the case of Exodus 19, we know who the *priests* are — the whole nation of Israel. We know who *God* is; He never changes. The question that must be asked is this: *Who are the people?* Who are the people that this new nation of priests was intended to serve?

The answer is that the nation of Israel was to serve as priests for all the other nations and peoples in the world! The Gentile (non-Jewish) nations were the only other people that a kingdom of priests could serve. God was unveiling a new step in the fulfillment of His great promise to Abraham: "...all peoples on earth will be blessed through you" (Gen 12:3b).

When God named Israel as a kingdom of priests, He was giving Israel a new identity. Now Israelites could not live for themselves alone; they were to be a holy people, separated to God's purpose. They were to serve between God and the nations to connect these two groups in covenant relationship!

The New Testament tells us that we in the church have inherited this ministry today. Consider the words of Peter and Paul. According to the writings of these apostles, we now have a priestly calling and duty. The church is to be a kingdom of priests for the nations. Peter says to those who have believed,

> *But you are a chosen people,*
> *a royal priesthood,*
> *a holy nation, a people belonging to God,*
> *that you may declare the praises of him*
> *who called you out of darkness into his wonderful light*
> *(1 Peter 2:9).*

Paul says of his own calling that God's purpose was for him to be

> *... a minister of Christ Jesus to the Gentiles*
> *with the priestly duty*
> *of proclaiming the gospel of God,*
> *so that the Gentiles might become an offering acceptable to God...*
> *(Romans 15:16a).*

Just like the children of Abraham, we in Christ's church have a very great calling. How wonderful to see God's wisdom and power as He acts to bring blessing to all nations! Let us pause for a moment to praise the Lord!

Prayer # 3

Almighty God,
We are humbled to see how You have remembered us.
When we were far from You, You were acting to bring us near.
Truly it is not we who have found You, but You who have found us!
Thank You for creating a Kingdom of Priests.
Thank You that You still call men, women, and children
to set them apart for Your higher purpose.
May we be willing to stand in the middle:
You on one side,
the nations on the other,
and we, the Kingdom of Priests, in the middle
speaking for You to the people
and teaching the people how to serve You.
In Jesus' name we pray,
Amen!

Figure 3.1

Summary

You have seen that Creation is the work of God and that all He has made is good, including people who are created in His image. Although people have fallen into sin, they are responsible for their sins. God could do away with people, but instead He chooses to redeem them because the nations and languages matter to God. Finally, God will act to bless every nation on earth through the family of one man — Abraham.

There are two lessons to learn from the fact that people are made in God's image: all of them can know God, and all of them can represent Him.

God's judgments are meant to redeem. They may convince the person who is punished to confess. If the person will not confess, God's punishments may make such an example of that person that other people who hear of it may repent of their sins before it is too late. God's ultimate intent for punishment is to redeem.

God gave the nations a covenant — a promise agreement in which two parties willingly agree to requirements in order to form a lasting relationship.

Review and Application

Now that you have completed your study of chapter 3, you should ask questions about the implications of your study for your ministry and/or Christian service.

1. Has God given you any promises that you are still waiting to see fulfilled? What kingdom-oriented dreams has He given to you?

2. Can the One Eternal God cease to exist? If not, then what does this teach us about God's covenant promises to Abraham?

3. How many parties (groups) are involved in the work of a priest? Explain.

4. How could Israel serve a priestly ministry for Gentile nations?

Be prepared to discuss these questions and any other questions or issues that come to mind when your instructor refers to them in class.

Unit 2
The Institution of the Missio Dei

C h a p t e r   4   –   Joshua's: three principles for all who desire to share in the mission of God; the principles of presence, blessing, and allocation in Joshua's experience under the leading of the Holy Spirit; and how these principles can shape the focus and activity of churches and their leaders today

C h a p t e r   5   –   Examples of the *Missio Dei* in the developing history of the people of Israel; God's call to His disobedient people to return to His mission after their disobedience to Him; God moves His plan for blessing the nations forward — even in times of difficulty and failure

C h a p t e r   6   –   The benefits of living in God's kingdom according to Wisdom Literature; life in the kingdom attractive because it works; the practicality of the wisdom of God for His covenant people; and how such wisdom causes the nations to desire to know the one true God

CHAPTER 4

The Principles
of God's Mission in Joshua

The Kingdom of God and the People of Israel

When God promised to use Abraham's family to bless all nations, He also promised that kings would come from Abraham.

> *Abram fell facedown, and God said to him,*
> *"As for me, this is my covenant with you:*
> *You will be the father of many nations.*
> *No longer will you be called Abram;*
> *your name will be Abraham…*
> *I will make you very fruitful;*
> *I will make nations of you,*
> ***and kings will come from you…***
> *(Genesis 17:3-6; emphasis mine).*

God was revealing to Abraham that His promise to bless all nations would involve a kingdom. This was a revelation of something new in God's plan.

Understanding the Kingdom of God

The kingdom of God is a major theme in the Bible. Kingdom involves the *authority to rule* (moral right). It also involves the *power to rule* (actual ability). Kingdom last of all involves the *scope of rule* (area of effective control).

Any kingdom that lacks one of these three qualities is incomplete:

- A kingdom that has power to rule and the scope of rule but lacks the authority (moral right) to rule is a tyranny or dictatorship.
- A kingdom that has authority to rule and scope of rule but lacks the power to rule is a weak kingdom with inadequate protection for its subjects.
- A kingdom with authority to rule and power to rule but no actual area of rule is a kingdom in name only, a kingdom in exile.

In the Bible, God announces His claim as rightful King of the world and all who live in it. God is neither a false dictator of the earth nor is He a weak king, and He is not a king in exile. Our God is indeed the rightful and powerful King of the whole earth!

The doctrine of Creation implies God's right to be King of all the earth:

- God is the personal Creator of all that has been made; so He has the *authority* to rule.
- God created everything by His word and will alone; so He has the *power* to rule.
- God created all things everywhere; so the *scope* of His rule includes the whole inhabited earth.

A Great King is on the Throne!

In the Old Testament, the kingdom of God was first established in a limited way. God founded an actual earthly kingdom. The kingdom was made up of the children of Abraham in the land of Canaan.

Later, God expanded His kingdom. Since New Testament days, God's kingdom includes the spiritual children of Abraham in the church around the world. A great King is on the throne!

In the letter to the Colossians, the apostle Paul clearly stated God's claims of kingship as he wrote under the inspiration of the Holy Spirit. He wanted to make the Colossian believers (and us) more aware of the kingly claims of Jesus Christ, which involved:

> *. . . giving thanks to the Father, who has qualified you*
> *to share in the inheritance of the saints **in the kingdom of light.***
> *For he has rescued us from the dominion of darkness*
> *and brought us **into the kingdom of the Son** He loves,*
> *in whom we have redemption, the forgiveness of sins.*
> *He is the image of the invisible God,*
> *the firstborn over all creation.*
> *For by him all things were created:*
> *things in heaven and on earth,*
> *visible or invisible,*
> *whether thrones or powers or rulers or authorities;*
> *all things were created by him and for him.*
> *He is before all things,*
> *and in him all things hold together.*
> *And he is the head of the body, the church;*
> *he is the beginning and the firstborn from among the dead,*
> *so that in everything he might have the supremacy*
> *(Colossians 1:12-18; emphasis mine).*

How important it is to know that our God is the great King over all the earth! A king does not have to ask for permission to act; he expects to be obeyed. A king will not allow imposters to take over parts of his kingdom. A good king has the best interests of his people at heart. We have such a King over us.

God's People Needed a Homeland

The people of God's new kingdom first of all needed a homeland in which to base. God provides for that in His covenant promises to Abraham, as well.

> *The whole land of Canaan, where you are now an alien,*
> *I will give as an everlasting possession to you*
> *and your descendents after you;*
> *and I will be their God*
> *(Genesis 17:8).*

God's promise-plan to bless the nations would involve kingdom. God planned to give Israel the land of the Canaanites. The book of Joshua tells the story of how the Israelites received their land and began to become the kingdom that God intended.

Joshua: Winning the Land for the Kingdom of God

The book of Joshua continues the account begun in the Pentateuch. Since Moses was about to die, he would not enter the Promised Land. So God called a new man to lead the people, and he had an enormous job. He had to replace Moses, Israel's great leader and deliverer. He also had to conquer Canaan, a land filled with strong, wicked people.

> *Then Moses went out and spoke these words to all Israel:*
> *"I am now a hundred and twenty years old*
> *and I am no longer able to lead you…*
> *The Lord your God himself will cross over ahead of you.*
> *He will destroy these nations before you,*
> *and you will take possession of their land.*
> *Joshua also will cross over ahead of you…"*
> *(Deuteronomy 31:1-2a, 3).*

After telling the people that Joshua would become their leader, Moses gave Joshua some specific instructions about his mission:

> *Then Moses summoned Joshua and said to him in the presence of all Israel,*
> *"Be strong and courageous, for you must go with this people*
> *into the land that the Lord swore to their forefathers to give to them,*
> *and you must divide it among them as their inheritance.*
> *The Lord himself goes before you and will be with you;*
> *he will never leave you nor forsake you.*
> *Do not be afraid; do not be discouraged"*
> *(Deuteronomy 31:7-8).*

What About the Canaanites?

Joshua was commanded to lead the people into their inheritance; however, other nations already lived there. It is important to answer the question of why Israel was authorized to attack and destroy the Canaanite nations. Was not Israel created to be a blessing to the nations? Why then were Israelites sent to attack and destroy the nations of Canaan? There are three answers to this question.

First of all, God made the world. As Creator and King, He has the right to divide His creation and give it to anyone He chooses.

Second, the Bible describes the nations of Canaan as societies that were ripe for judgment. Long before, God had told Abraham, "In the fourth generation your descendants will come back here, for the sin of the Amorites has not yet reached its full measure" (Genesis 15:16). At that time, God did not allow Abraham to attack the Amorites in Canaan.

Four hundred years later, the descendants of the Amorites had fallen into wickedness, immorality, and human sacrifice. In Leviticus 18:28, God told Moses that the land of Canaan "vomited out" these nations. The land, created by a holy God, could not tolerate their behavior.

God authorized the destruction of these people because they would not change their evil ways. God's judgments are redemptive in nature, either to those punished or to those who observe. If the Canaanites would no longer respond to God, then God would give their land to other people who would listen.

Third, the same passage warns Israelites that if they defiled the land, they also would be "vomited out" of it. God would not tolerate such serious sin in the land He had created. This warning later came true when the Israelites were taken from the land in captivity to Assyria and Babylon.

These three facts show us that God was not unjust or inconsistent in sending Israel to destroy the Canaanite nations and take their land. A wicked and unresponsive people were to be replaced by a people that would obey God. The Israelites would teach others to serve God, too.

The land of God's enemies would become the land of God's kingdom of priests. Joshua was the man who would lead the people into their inheritance.

> *After the death of Moses the servant of the Lord,*
> *The Lord said to Joshua son of Nun, Moses' aide:*
> *"Moses my servant is dead.*
> *Now then, you and all these people,*
> *get ready to cross the Jordan River*
> *into the land I am about to give to them — to the Israelites"*
> *(Joshua 1:1-2).*

The 'Joshua Commission'

Joshua faced many difficult decisions after Moses died. How could he lead God's people to take the land? The Jordan River separated God's people from the land. The Israelites did not have military training or equipment, but the Canaanites had both. The Canaanites also had strong cities with fortified walls.

To help Joshua face these challenges, God gave him the following soul-stirring promises:

> *I will give you every place where you set your foot, as I promised Moses.*
> *Your territory will extend...*
> *No one will be able to stand up against you all the days of your life.*
> *As I was with Moses, so I will be with you;*
> *I will never leave you nor forsake you.*
> *Be strong and courageous, because you will lead these people*
> *to inherit the land I swore to their forefathers to give them.*
> *Be strong and very courageous*
> *(Joshua 1: 3-4a, 5-7a).*

Not only did God give Joshua encouragement, He also gave him specific instructions about how he was to prepare for a lifetime of leadership. The key was to listen to God by meditating on His Word. Joshua was instructed to live a life shaped by daily humble interaction with the Word of God.

> *Be careful to obey all the law my servant Moses gave you;*
> *do not turn from it to the right or to the left,*
> *that you may be successful wherever you go.*
> *Do not let this Book of the Law depart from your mouth;*
> *meditate on it day and night,*

> *so that you may be careful to do everything written in it.*
> *Then you will be prosperous and successful*
> *(Joshua 1:7b-8).*

Joshua was to spend the rest of his life growing ever more familiar with God's Word. He was told to do this by reading the Word, meditating on it, speaking about it, and obeying it. He was not to wander to any extreme position, right or left. He was to obey it all.

Remembering God's Word is the first step in obeying God. God told Joshua that success would come to him as he meditated on God's words, obeyed them, and trusted in the active presence of God.

Joshua had to be close to God because God had planned a great work for His people. God commanded the Israelites to take the land of promise. God was opening a door for them to enter. As the King, God has the right to move His people if He so desires.

The Kingdom of God Progresses Forward

In God's new plan, His people were not to stay where they were. Since they were God's moveable possession, they must advance forward according to His will. God wanted His people to be at work with Him in the fulfillment of His plan.

> *Now Jericho was tightly shut up because of the Israelites.*
> *No one went out and no one came in.*
> *Then the Lord said to Joshua,*
> *"See, I have delivered Jericho into your hands,*
> *along with its king and its fighting men"*
> *(Joshua 6:1-2).*

The first city Joshua encountered in Canaan was Jericho. The city was a great walled fortress whose walls were too thick to break and too high to climb. The only way in or out was through the city gates, and these gates were locked and guarded.

Joshua noticed the closed doors of Jericho; however, God saw things differently. God said that the doors to Jericho (and to all the Promised Land) were open!

God's open doors are meant to be entered! God's way of seeing opportunity may be different from our way, for He may say a door is open even when there is opposition. Challenges that look impossible to us are not impossible to God.

If we are in covenant with Almighty God, we can confidently approach the doors that He tells us are open. We do not advance in our own ability because the manifest presence of God goes with us. It is our covenant relationship with God that makes the difference.

Joshua's Three Principles for the People who Obey God's Mission

The book of Joshua teaches three major principles for a people in covenant with the God of mission:

- God's manifest presence accompanies those who advance toward His kingdom goals according to His will.
- All true victories in the kingdom of God are done with the blessing of the nations in view.
- It is necessary to allocate kingdom tasks to God's people and make the people accountable for their completion.

These principles from Joshua can be applied to our lives and ministries today (York, 33-37).

Principle #1 — *God's manifest presence accompanies those who advance toward His kingdom goals according to His will.*

God's will was to lead the people of Israel into the promised land of Canaan. This in turn would open the way for the establishment of the kingdom that would ultimately exist to bless all nations. God was sending the people into Canaan. If the people obeyed God and entered Canaan, they could expect God's presence to be with them in visible ways. God's manifest presence would be with them as they advanced according to His will!

> *Have I not commanded you?*
> *Be strong and courageous.*
> *Do not be terrified; do not be discouraged,*
> *for the Lord your God will be with you wherever you go*
> *(Joshua 1:9).*

The idea of God being with His people is an important theme in Joshua and in the whole Bible. Israel's battles were fought with untrained men and inferior equipment. Since the Israelite soldiers did not even have war chariots, they could only win battles against the Canaanites if God were with them. Yet they did win the victory! Israel's victories were clear, observable signs of God's presence with them.

Israel's victories were clear signs of God's manifest presence with them!

God's words here in the Old Testament to Joshua are a preview of what God would say again in the New Testament to the church. God also gave us a seemingly impossible mission:

> *Then Jesus came to them and said,*
> *"All authority in heaven and on earth has been given to me.*
> *Therefore go and make disciples of all nations,*
> *baptizing them in the name of the Father and of the Son and of the Holy Spirit,*
> *and teaching them to obey everything I have commanded you"*
> *(Matthew 28:18-20a).*

God also told us that He would be with us to see that the victory is won:

> *"And surely I am with you always, to the very end of the age"*
> *(Matthew 28:20b).*

Remember: in any age, people called by God to do His purpose can be sure that God's manifest presence will go with them. Those advancing on God's mission are never alone. God's presence with us is the greatest encouragement we can ever have!

Principle #2 — *All true victories in the kingdom of God are done with the blessing of the nations in view.*

Look closely at this passage from the third chapter of Joshua. The story concerns the miraculous crossing of the Jordan River. The river was flooded; yet God caused the water to stop flowing so that the Israelites could cross into their Promised Land. This was a mighty demonstration of the manifest presence of God with them.

> Joshua said to the Israelites,
> "Come here and listen to the words of the Lord your God.
> This is how you will know that the living God is among you
> and that he will certainly drive out before you the Canaanites...
> See, the ark of the covenant
> **of the Lord of all the earth**
> will go into the Jordan ahead of you...
> And as soon as the priests who carry the ark of the Lord —
> **the Lord of all the earth —**
> set foot in the Jordan,
> its waters flowing downstream will be cut off and stand up in a heap"
> (Joshua 3:9-10a, 11, 13; emphasis mine).

It is interesting to hear the words of the Lord here. He was speaking to Israel, but twice He made it clear that He was God of the whole earth. It was "the Lord of all the earth" who caused the water to stop flowing and stand in a heap.

This repeated phrase "the Lord of all the earth" should cause us to pay attention. God is not merely a local deity; He is God everywhere. His authority extends over the whole earth. The God who spoke to Israelites at Mount Sinai could also speak to them in Canaan. The God who parted the Red Sea in Egypt could also part the Jordan River in Canaan. This God has authority in your situation as well.

The "Lord of all the earth" wants to bless all nations.

Israelites were obeying the one true God, the Lord of all the earth. He should rightfully be worshipped by all nations. Israel's victories took place so that everyone could know about the one true Lord, "the Lord of all the earth." God repeats this truth many times in Scripture.

This powerful lesson is repeated a third time after the people crossed over the Jordan. God explains very clearly here why He performed this unusual and outstanding miracle. Joshua set up a memorial marker on the Canaanite side of the river and then explained its meaning to the Israelites:

> *The Lord your God did to the Jordan*
> *just what He had done to the Red Sea*
> *when He dried it up before us until we had crossed over.*
> **He did this so that all the peoples of the earth might know**
> *that the hand of the Lord is powerful*
> *and so that you might always fear the Lord your God*
> *(Joshua 4:23-24; emphasis mine).*

Joshua's God was not just the God of blessing for the Israelites; He was the God of the whole earth. When the Israelites won victories and advanced, the blessing of all nations was kept in view.

Principle # 3 — *It is necessary to allocate kingdom tasks to God's people and make the people accountable for their completion.*

Most of the remainder of the book of Joshua explains in detail how Joshua assigned the task of taking and dividing the land. Earlier, Moses had commissioned Joshua to do this:

> *Then Moses summoned Joshua*
> *and said to him in the presence of all Israel,*
> *"Be strong and courageous, for you must go with this people*
> *into the land that the Lord swore to their forefathers to give them,*
> *and you must divide it among them as their inheritance"*
> *(Deuteronomy 31:7).*

Moses had made Joshua accountable for the division of the land into inheritance parcels. He did this by giving Joshua this command in the presence of all Israel. Now Joshua in turn held the people publicly accountable for winning and dividing the land. This process is called *allocation*.

Allocation is a process of public accountability to finish a task.

After the first victories in Joshua's military campaigns (chapters 6-12), many areas still remained to be taken:

> *When Joshua was old and well advanced in years,*
> *the Lord said to him, "You are very old,*
> *and there are still very large areas of land to be taken over…*
> *Be sure to allocate this land to Israel for an inheritance,*
> *as I have instructed you…"*
> *(Joshua 13:1, 6b).*

Joshua's response to God's instructions is seen in chapter 18:

> *So Joshua said to the Israelites:*
> *"How long will you wait before you begin to take possession of the land*
> *that the Lord, the God of your fathers, has given you?*
> ***Appoint*** *three men from each tribe.*
> *I will **send** them out to make a **survey** of the land*
> *and to **write** a description of it,*
> *according to the inheritance of each.*
> *Then they will **return** to me.*
> *You are to **divide** the land into seven parts…"*
> *(Joshua 18:3-5a; emphasis mine).*

Notice the six actions (verbs) that Joshua commanded the people to do:

Appoint	**Send**	**Survey**
Write	**Return**	**Divide**

Joshua appointed responsible men and sent them out to make a survey of the unfinished task. He required them to write a description of what they found, and he directed them to return and report what they had discovered. He required them to divide the total unfinished task into smaller sections. These are actions that church leaders must take, as well.

This fact-finding process was not the end of what Joshua did. He also required the surveyors to report back. Then he acted on the basis of their report.

> *"After you have written descriptions of the seven parts of the land,*
> *bring them here to me*
> *and I will cast lots for you in the presence of the Lord our God…"*
> *So the men left and went through the land.*

> *They wrote its description on a scroll,*
> *town by town, in seven parts,*
> *and returned to Joshua in the camp at Shiloh.*
> *Joshua then cast lots for them in Shiloh in the presence of the Lord,*
> *and there **he distributed the land** to the Israelites*
> *according to their tribal divisions*
> *(Joshua 18:6, 9-10; emphasis mine).*

Joshua allocated the work that needed to be done, and then he sent out workers to study the unfinished task. The surveyors divided each task into subtasks. A separate subtask was then allocated (assigned) to each tribe for completion.

Applying the Principle of Allocation in the Church

Today, believers in the church can learn a lesson by thinking about the principles found in Joshua. When God gives us a task to do in His kingdom, He expects us to manage it well. The leadership of the church should also identify the total task to be accomplished. Leaders may also need to assign survey agents to travel, study, and write down the description of the remaining task.

Agents that study the unfinished task of the church are sent to answer several practical questions. They study human populations, including age, population density, where people live, and how they earn their living. This study concerns what we refer to as *demographics*. These agents also study the spiritual need and lost condition of groups of people. This is an early step in the ministry of evangelism.

Studying the Unfinished Task

The work of such agents, then, could be described as *Evangelism Demographics*. An effective church or national church office may use such agents. The church planning office should be a place of prayer. It may also have a map with zones and markers on it.

The leadership team uses the work of the "evangelism demographers." Team members also fast and pray to get the guidance of the Holy Spirit on where and how to expand the work of the gospel. They ask questions such as the following:

Our City

- How many neighborhoods or zones are in our city?
- How many of them are unreached?
- What age, sex, or economic groups in our area do not have a significant outreach targeted to them?
- Who are the "invisible people" in our neighborhoods?
- Are there any people in our city who would not feel comfortable attending our existing church (or churches)?
- What languages are commonly heard in our neighborhood but are rarely heard in our church?

Our Area

- How many towns and villages in our area do not have a church?
- Where in our country are there people who do not have a church within walking distance of their home?
- Are there any major professions in our area that are not represented in our church (taxi drivers, fishermen, soldiers, traders, farmers)?
- What other language groups live around us?
- Do these neighboring language groups each have a biblical, Spirit-filled church or missionary at this time?
- If so, what are we doing to support this church or missionary?
- If not, what does God want us to do about this?

Our Nation

- What unreached tribes or peoples live near our nation?
- Are there any people groups living in our region who do not know that Jesus is King over all the earth?
- Is anything being done to evangelize the followers of other world religions living in our area?
- When God looks at our part of the world, what completely unreached groups of people does He see?
- What can we do to evangelize and disciple these groups?
- Where has God opened the doors of missions to us today?

Responding to the Unfinished Task

After answering questions like these, the leaders should prayerfully divide the total task into separate parts. Each part should then be allotted to a person or group in the church.

There must be prayer and training for these workers. After some time has passed, each responsible group in the church should report back to the leaders about how their part of the task is progressing.

One of the best resources available to leaders for seeing the unfinished task around the world is an unusual book titled *Operation World* by Patrick Johnstone. *Operation World* is actually a prayer calendar for each day of the year. Every day at least one nation of the world is discussed. The daily reading gives valuable information about the needs and opportunities in the kingdom of God around the world.

What a blessing it is to lead God's people in regular, well-informed prayer for the nations of the world! A leader who commits to lead his or her people in this prayer discipline will be rewarded by having a people of vision to lead in the future.

The Spiritual Nature of Planning for the Unfinished Task

Someone might question whether Spirit-filled Christians need to organize God's work. This is a good question.

People are made in the image of God (Genesis 1:27), and they are capable of representing Him. Adam was capable of the great task of identifying and naming the animals. His job of taxonomy required organizational ability. People whom God calls to spread the gospel are also capable of doing good organizational work.

No organizational plan should be held as "sacred" by itself. If God redirects His people, they should obey and change their plan.

However, if we make no clear plan for doing God's kingdom business, we may fail to complete it. Then we will give an account to God for our stewardship of His great mission. He will also require an account of the many resources He gave us to work with. Jesus taught this principle as well:

> *A man of noble birth went to a distant country*
> *to have himself appointed king and then to return.*
> *So he called ten of his servants and gave them ten minas*
> *[a mina was about three months' wages].*
> *"Put this money to work," he said, "until I come back"…*
> *He was made king… and returned home.*
> *Then he sent for the servants to whom he had given the money,*
> *in order to find out what they had gained with it.*
>
> *The first one came and said,*
> *"Sir, your mina has earned ten more."*
> *"Well done, my good servant!" his master replied.*
> *"Because you have been trustworthy in a very small matter,*
> *take charge of ten cities."*
> *The second came and said,*
> *"Sir, your mina has earned five more."*
> *His master answered, "You take charge of five cities."*
>
> *Then another servant came and said,*
> *"Sir, here is your mina;*
> *I have kept it laid away in a piece of cloth…"*
> *His master replied,*
> *"I will judge you by your own words, you wicked servant…*
> *Why … didn't you put my money on deposit,*
> *so that when I came back, I could have collected it with interest?"*
> *(Luke 19:12-13, 15-21a, 22-23).*

The third servant had no plan to account for the investment his master entrusted to him. He only arranged to return his master's investment unused. The master judged this to be unacceptable, and he called the third man a wicked servant.

According to verse 11, Jesus told this parable while He was at the house of a man named Zacchaeus who had been a corrupt tax collector. He had just repented and gladly announced his new plan. Zacchaeus planned to serve God by giving to the poor and by paying back extra money to the people he had cheated. Jesus approved of this kind of Spirit-motivated planning.

Jesus' story is very clear. God is entrusting us with His mission and His resources. He has given us a meaningful mission, people to lead, physical resources, and spiritual anointing. He expects us to plan for ways to use them for His glory. We will give an account for our use of His gifts!

> *The third servant had no plan to account for the investment his master entrusted to him.*

The Issue of Developing Workers for the Unfinished Task

Another key question is how to find the manpower to do such a great task. The answer to this is that the minister must learn to give the ministry away!

God entrusts individuals and groups of His people with specific missions that contribute to the great *Missio Dei*. Like Joshua, we must be willing to accept our own responsibility. If He allows us to lead others, we also must delegate important tasks to the people we lead. Our delegation must be specific enough that each person knows what he or she is to do and when to do it.

If we do not give the people important tasks to do, they may grow discouraged or idle. If either of these things happens, the people will fail to enter their inheritance! The Israelites would not have been prepared to cross the Jordan if Joshua had not ordered them to get ready.

Believers are not to be gathered into one place and hoarded. They are to be healed and equipped and then sent out into their world to work for God!

The goal of church leadership is to help each believer find his or her God-given job(s) in the kingdom. Every person God saves has a God-given gift. Christian leaders are called by God to help all believers use their gifts effectively and in harmony.

> But to **each one of us** grace has been given
> as Christ apportioned it…It was He who gave
> some to be apostles,
> some to be prophets,
> some to be evangelists, and
> some to be pastors and teachers,
> to prepare God's people for works of service,
> so that the body of Christ may be built up…
> (Ephesians 4:7, 11-12; emphasis mine).

Good Christian leadership does not try to hold God's people back. This passage in Ephesians says that ministers are to prepare all of God's people for works of service. Good Christian leadership surveys the unfinished task and gives important jobs to each Christian to fulfill. Every Christian should be "spiritually employed" in the work of God!

This does not mean that every Christian is called to be financially supported as a minister. It does mean that every single believer in Jesus is gifted to do an important job in fulfilling Christ's mission.

God did not design His church as a "Members-Only Club." Instead, He created it as a "Spiritual Employment Agency!"

Problems that Keep the Church from Responding to the Unfinished Task

In most local churches or groups of churches, two organizational factors hinder the work of evangelism, church growth, and missions. These factors are the lack of a clear one-on-one discipleship plan and the lack of money to support the work. If workers are not developed, and if there is no effort to finance the work, then the work will usually stay unfinished.

Church leaders can ask some additional questions to face these common organizational barriers.

Our Disciples

- Do we have a plan for discipling new believers?
- Has this plan ever been written down?
- If a new believer were successfully discipled in our church…
  …what would this person be able to *do*?
  …what would this person *know*?

...how would he or she *be involved* in the church's ministries?

- How will our disciples learn to do these things, to know this information, and to become involved in this way?
- Do we have workers responsible for putting this discipleship plan into action?
- Are the workers who are responsible for discipleship trained and supported?
- Are the workers aware of the schedule when they will report on the progress of their disciples?
- Are the leaders aware of how to assist and encourage the workers?
- How will we know if we have reached our discipleship goals or not?

Our Funding

- How many of our people (or churches, ministers, etc.) give a *regular* offerings (beyond tithes) to fund the evangelism, discipleship, and missions ministries of the church?
- How many of our people do *not* give regularly to this cause?
- Who is excluded from giving to God in the New Testament?
- How much money would be available to the work of God if everybody in our fellowship gave even a small percentage of their regular income (2-5%) to this work?
- If ten employed Christians tithe faithfully, can they support a pastor on their own income level?
- If twenty employed Christians gave an additional half-tithe, could they support the personal income of their own missionary?
- How can we, as leaders, model and encourage complete participation to make this financial miracle possible?

The Power of Teamwork for the Unfinished Task

Evangelism and funding are two important areas to plan for and work on regularly in the church. We tend to overestimate how much one person can do. However, we tend to underestimate how much the whole church can do — if everyone participates.

The church does not need just one dynamic worker nor does it need a rich donor. The church needs each of its people to be involved in God's work, using the gifts God has actually given them. Working together leads to a new integrity, God-given dignity, and great power.

Working together leads to integrity, dignity, and power.

The pyramids of Egypt were built by the power of thousands of hands working in well-organized unity. Each block of stone weighed several tons. Vast teams of simple laborers worked in unison and transported the stones for hundreds of miles across the land of Egypt. Then they raised the stones to amazing heights. Their results of their unified efforts can still be seen along the Nile River today, thousands of years later.

If enough hands act in unity, they can move a mountain. In the words of the proverb: *"Many hands make light work!"*

It is also necessary to teach the importance of reporting back to church leadership. After delegating a task, the leader must learn how to call for a report. Reports of ministry activity should be honest and specific. The ministry report should share the advances made as well as the difficulties encountered.

After the report is given the leader must provide an effective response. Words of encouragement, correction, new direction, and caring advice may need to be given. A wise leader uses encouragement much more often than rebuke!

Christian leaders must follow up on the reports given, as Joshua did. He was neither too involved nor too distant from the work he delegated to the people. They were required to act on their own, but they also could come to him for evaluation and encouragement when necessary.

Summary

Joshua obeyed God by leading His people into the Promised Land. From this homeland, Israel was to bless all nations in fulfillment of Abraham's Covenant. Joshua used three principles that can help others who desire to share in the mission of God. These are: 1) dependence on God's manifest presence, 2) awareness of the blessing of nations, and 3) the allocation of the unfinished task.

Review and Application

Now that you have completed your study of chapter 4, what effect will the principles of God's mission in Joshua have on your ministry and your personal and family life? May they give direction to your efforts and assurance as you apply them.

1. What was Joshua specifically instructed to do with the Word of God?

2. List at least five ways that reading the Word of God may bring spiritual blessing to a believer's life.

3. What encouragement could Joshua receive from God's promise to be with him as he went forward in God's will?

4. List three areas in your life in which you have advanced to obey the mission of God. How has God been with you as you have obeyed Him?

5. Have different members of the class read aloud the following verses. After reading each verse, discuss how it emphasizes the worldwide rule of God: Psalm 24:1, Isaiah 54:5, Jeremiah 10:7, Micah 4:13, Zephaniah 2:11, Zechariah 4:14.

6. Based on these verses, how must God feel today when He looks out at the earth and sees peoples who do not yet know about Him?

Be prepared to discuss these questions and any other questions or issues that may come to mind when your instructor refers to them in class.

CHAPTER 5

The Story of God's Mission in the Historical Books

Many of the books following the Pentateuch in the Bible are called "Historical Books." They tell the story of how God established and led the Israelites so that they could become the nation to bless all other nations. Sometimes the Israelites did well; often they failed. Yet God never gave up on His mission.

Joshua and Jesus: Models of Mission-Oriented Leadership

Joshua is a model of good leadership. He models a biblical, mission-oriented leadership style. He took responsibility for the overall task, but he did not attempt to do the whole task by himself. Instead, he mobilized all God's people to action, and he held them accountable. He surveyed the task, divided it into subtasks, allocated the work to be done, required reports, and acted on the reports given by the workers.

It is interesting to remember that Joshua shares his name with the greatest leader of all time. The name *Jesus* is a newer version of the Old Testament name *Joshua.*

Jesus was also a mission-oriented leader. He intended to finish the work given to Him by His Father. In fact, He completed His earthly work by the time He was thirty-three years old!

Jesus' ministry plan resembles the plan from God used by Joshua because both Jesus and Joshua received their part of the mission. Jesus also divided His task, equipped workers, sent them out, and received their reports. Furthermore, He expected His disciples to change the world. He lived His life with these disciples to show them how to do the work. He also equipped them with the power of the Holy Spirit.

Read the following verses and then study the chart entitled "The Leadership Methods of Joshua and Jesus:"

- For **Joshua**
    - → Deuteronomy 31:7-8
    - → Joshua 1:10-11
    - → Joshua 18:1-10

- For **Jesus**
    - → Luke 9:1-10
    - → *Luke 10:1-24*
    - → *Luke 24:45-49*
    - → *Acts 1:1-8*

The Leadership Methods of Joshua and Jesus	
Joshua...	*Jeusus...*
Was called to take the Land of Canaan	*Was called to redeem all nations*
Was sent to take all the land for God	*Was sent to redeem all nations for God*
Divided the task into parts (subtasks)	*Sent His disciples to witness in separate areas*
Focused on mobilizing the 12 tribes	*Focused on making 12 disciples*

Delegated the work to teams from the tribes	*Delegated the work to teams of disciples*
Required detailed reports from the tribes	*Required detailed reports from the disciples*
Listened to the surveyors' reports	*Listened to the disciples' reports*
Urged leaders to finish the work	*Commissioned His disciples to finish the work*
Depended on the power of God for victory	*Depended on the Holy Spirit for victory*

Figure 5.1

The examples of Jesus and Joshua should be a practical help and an inspiration to every Christian leader. These examples can help us to grow in the ability to *"prepare God's people for works of service"* (Ephesians 4:12a).

The book of Joshua shows us the picture of a leader and a people who intended to obey God's command. They took God seriously and organized themselves for obedience. God was giving them a homeland from which they would bless all nations. They were about to occupy the land of their inheritance!

Judges and Ruth: The Kingdom in Difficult Times

In Judges, we read of the early failures of Israel. During this time, the people had no human king over them. Left to themselves, the people slipped into sin and godlessness; so God allowed oppressors to abuse them. When they began to pray and repent of their sin, God provided a leader or *judge* to deliver them from the oppressors.

The people were first obedient and then disobedient. During the good years, Israel showed the world that it was desirable to live inside of the covenant relationship with God. During the bad years, God's judgments on Israel taught the ungodly nations that life outside of God's covenant protection was not worth living. Tragically, the sins of the people grew worse as time went on.

Gideon's Declaration

In the middle of the book of Judges is the central story of Gideon. Although Gideon is best known for defeating the army of Midian by obeying God, the high point of his life came after this battle. When the people wanted to make Gideon or his son their king, he refused. He declared that Israel was still God's kingdom — a nation that existed to obey God's plan — and so only God could be their king:

> **"I will not rule** over you,
> **nor will my son rule** over you.
> **The Lord will rule** over you"
> *(Judges 8:23; emphasis mine).*

Even in dark times, God's kingdom is still alive. Gideon's declaration shows the mercy of God and indicates that He would not give up on the people of Israel.

Ruth's Declaration

Ruth is a small but amazing book, and it is also a great poetic love story. Even the number of words are counted and balanced artistically in the Hebrew text (see the NIV Study Bible, Introduction: Ruth). Ideas are balanced, names have meaning, vivid language is used, and wordplays make the writing beautiful.

However, there is more in Ruth than beautiful writing. The theology of the *Missio Dei* is also present, for it tells the story of a young lady from another nation who is included in the blessings of God's kingdom!

Ruth is from the neighboring nation of Moab. She did not grow up serving the one true God. She became a young widow before ever bearing a child. However, in spite of her family tragedy and her foreign background, God sees her desire to know Him. Ruth shared her desire with her Israelite mother-in-law, Naomi:

> *But Ruth replied,*
> *"Don't urge me to leave you*
> *or to turn back from you.*

> *Where you go I will go,*
> *and where you stay I will stay.*
> *Your people will be my people*
> *and your God my God"*
> *(Ruth 1:16).*

Ruth the Moabite widow made a powerful declaration here about her faith in God. She wanted the God of Naomi the Israelite to also be the God of Ruth the Moabite. Ruth was considering the kingdom of God and wondering if her nation could be blessed as well!

Ruth wondered if her nation could be blessed, as well!

God saw Ruth's desire to serve Him and accepted her. He brought her into His covenant people through her thrilling marriage to a godly Israelite, Boaz. Ruth not only joined the Hebrew people but also became an important person in God's plan for Israel. Amazingly, this sincere foreign woman became the great-grandmother of King David!

David is the man God used to rescue Israel from the dark period of the Judges. To be David's great-grandmother was a great blessing; however, Ruth was given an even greater honor than this. God included Ruth in the lineage of David's most important descendant — the most important baby ever born — Jesus Christ Himself.

God's Declaration

Like Ruth, we who seek God today may also be included in God's covenant people in spite of our past. Christ redeems us from sin, and God makes a declaration that changes the story of our lives forever:

> *Therefore, if anyone is in Christ, he is a new creation;*
> *the old has gone, the new has come!*
> *(2 Corinthians 5:17).*

Since God has declared that He is willing to accept "foreigners" into His kingdom, it is important to consider whether churches are as accepting as God is. Sometimes people who are culturally different from Christians do not feel welcome or accepted by Christians. Churches sometimes find it hard to change customs or to create new ministries so that culturally different people may learn to worship God with them.

Naomi decided to let Ruth accompany her back to Israel after she saw the sincerity of Ruth's heart. She shared her life, her fellowship, her food, her future destiny, and even her faith with this young Moabite woman. Perhaps the church should ask itself: "Does our church welcome people of other cultures as readily as Naomi welcomed Ruth?"

May the church today also decide to include the foreigner God sets before us.

Naomi had many problems of her own. It was not convenient for her to take care of another woman. At first she did not plan to open her heart to Ruth; however, in time she allowed God to change her plans. Eventually, Naomi cooperated with God and welcomed Ruth the Moabitess into her circle of friendship.

Prayer #4

Almighty God,
How wonderful are Your love and mercy!
We pray to You in reverence, for You are great;
but we also pray to You in delight, for You are kind and gracious.
Thank You for caring for us!
Thank You for changing the story of our lives!
Thank You for putting us in Your wonderful family!
Thank You for making everything new!
Truly we have much to celebrate.
You see us with eyes of mercy.
Help us see one another with mercy, too!
In Jesus' wonderful Name,
Amen.

Figure 5.2

Because of Naomi's obedience, she eventually lived to see her grandchildren and to be a part of the family from which King David and Jesus Himself would come. Naomi's decision to include the foreigner meant that she played a part in advancing the *Missio Dei!* May the church today also decide to include the foreigner God sets before it.

The darkness of the book of Judges and the bright light of the poetic story of Ruth both show us that God is still king. He is able to rescue those who sincerely call on Him. Those whom He rescues, He blesses beyond all measure, and He places them in his own eternal family. The old is gone and everything is made new!

David's Throne: The Kingdom Covenant

In the books of 1 Samuel and 2 Samuel the account of David is told. King David's rule is the high point of the political kingdom of Israel. Both 1 and 2 Kings and 1 and 2 Chronicles tell the ongoing story of the "kingdom of David."

In terms of the *Missio Dei,* God was beginning to fulfill the covenant promise to Abraham that "kings will come from you" (Genesis 17:6). David's kingdom had a purpose. It was established to fulfill the greatest promise of Abraham's covenant: "all peoples on earth will be blessed through you" (Genesis 12:3b).

God moved Israel past the difficult period of the Judges by raising up kings who were supposed to rule wisely. These kings were exhorted to know the Word of God. By studying God's Word, they were supposed to lead God's people in fulfilling God's mission to bless the nations around them. Although Saul was the first king of Israel, he disobeyed God; so the Covenant Kingdom is established first with David.

The Covenant with David

David had a tender heart for God. Scripture shows that God loved David's desire to be obedient and responsive. Like Joshua, David's life was shaped by meditation on God's Word. Although 2 Samuel 7 is the least-known of the important Old Testament covenants, it records a dramatic conversation between God and David.

David became king many years after he was anointed by the prophet Samuel. God established and expanded David's kingdom to include all of Israel. David defeated his enemies by God's power and established his capital city in Jerusalem. He even built a new palace, but something felt wrong in David's heart. How could he live in a palace when the ark of God was still kept in a tent?

> *After the king was settled in his palace*
> *and the Lord had given him rest from all his enemies around him,*
> *he said to Nathan the prophet,*
> *"Here I am, living in a palace of cedar,*
> *while the ark of God remains in a tent"*
> *(2 Samuel 7:1-2).*

David had a house (a palace) of his own, but he wanted to build another house (a temple) for God. At first, the prophet Nathan encouraged David to build this house for God; however, God sent Nathan back to deliver a different message to David that night. The first part of the covenant reviews what God has already done:

> *This is what the Lord says:*
> ***"Are you the one to build me a house** to live in?*
> *...I took you from the pasture and from following the flock*
> *to be ruler over my people Israel.*
> *I have been with you wherever you have gone,*
> *and I have cut off all your enemies from before you.*
> *Now I will make your name great,*
> *like the names of the greatest men of the earth.*
> *And I will provide a place for my people Israel*
> *and will plant them so that they can have a home of their own*
> *and no longer be disturbed...*
> *(2 Samuel 7:5b, 8-10a; emphasis mine).*

Up to this point, God's covenant with David is like the previous covenant with Abraham. God has chosen a man and He has made his name great. He will use David to provide Israel with a safe homeland; however, the second part of David's covenant promise from God is different. Here is something new in the history of God's covenants.

> The Lord declares to you that
> **the Lord himself will establish a house for you:**
> *When your days are over and you rest with your fathers,*
> *I will raise up your offspring to succeed you,*
> *who will come from your own body,*
> *and I will establish his kingdom.*
> *He is the one who will build a house for My Name,*
> *and I will establish the throne of his kingdom* **forever.**
> *I will be his father, and he will be my son…*
> *…my love will never be taken away from him…*
> **Your house and your kingdom will endure forever before me;**
> *your throne will be established forever*
> *(2 Samuel 7:11b-14a, 15a, 16; emphasis mine).*

David wanted to build God a house, but God said that David would not build him a house (temple). Instead, God would build David a house (a dynasty). Not only that, but this God-given dynasty would last forever.

The Power of the "Forever" Covenant

David was amazed at this wonderful new covenant. He was also humbled and thrilled to think that God would build his kingdom into a dynasty of kings. However, it was the word "forever" that amazed David most.

A "forever promise" can only be made by someone who is eternal. An old song once said, "Forever is a long, long time!" Actually, "forever" is longer than time.

The word "forever" is the most startling feature of the Davidic covenant. We may use the word "forever" to mean "a long time" or perhaps "the rest of our life." God never dies; so when God says "forever," He is pointing beyond time into eternity.

When God says "forever," He is pointing beyond time into eternity.

David's response was important. He felt that God's words to him were something new, a "torah" (a covenant or a charter) for all mankind!

> *Then King David went in and sat before the Lord, and he said:*
> *"Who am I, O Sovereign Lord,*
> *and what is my family,*
> *that you have brought me this far?*
> *And as if this were not enough in your sight, O Sovereign Lord,*
> *you have also spoken about the future of the house of your servant.*
> *Is this your usual way of dealing with man, O Sovereign Lord?*
> *…And now, Lord God, keep forever the promise you have made*
> *concerning your servant and his house.*
> *Do as you promised, so that your name will be great forever*
> *(2 Samuel 7:18-19, 25-26).*

The word "usual way" is "*torah*" in Hebrew which can also mean "teaching" or "charter." Here David tells God that he sees this "forever promise" as a new teaching or "charter" for mankind (Kaiser, 27). God is describing a new order in His relationship to man. All of mankind will be affected by this wonderful new covenant.

He will draw all nations to the worship of God in a Kingdom that lasts forever!

An eternal promise given to David by God must line up with the eternal promises God had made earlier to Abraham. Here, God is making it very clear that the promise to bless all nations (given to Abraham) will be fulfilled through a dynasty that lasts forever (given to David). No wonder David sat down in the presence of God in wonderful amazement!

The kings in the line of David were really vice-regents or lesser kings who represented the Sovereign Creator. This Creator had promised Abraham that He would make his family a kingdom of priests to bless all nations. Now, the kingdom was a reality.

David's earthly kingdom in Jerusalem did not last forever. Sin entered the kingly line and eventually destroyed the earthly kingdom. However, David's great Son will one day come and set up a kingdom that will never end. King Jesus is the fulfillment of the covenant made with David.

Summary

The historical books tell more than the story of the establishment of the nation of Israel. They also tell the story of the development of God's plan to bless all nations through the descendents of Abraham. Sometimes the story is grim with failure. At other times, the plans of God can be seen shining through the obedience of His people. God established David on the throne of Israel and promised him a kingdom that would last forever. Throughout the history of Israel, God never failed to advance the mission that He had committed to fulfill!

Review and Application

Now that you have completed the study of chapter 5, take time to reflect on the additional information you have gleaned about the mission of God in the Historical Books. The following questions help to focus your attention on this information.

1. Leaders must not be idle. However, they must not try to do the whole work by themselves, either. Why is this?

2. Joshua and Jesus both practiced delegation of tasks to other workers. What are you doing to "give away the work of the ministry" to other believers? How well have you performed the work that your leaders have delegated to you?

3. What was Ruth's declaration? How was God's treatment of Ruth an example of the ongoing progress of the Missio Dei?

4. Why was David so amazed by God's promise to "build him a house"?

5. Think about the way God moves through history. How has God moved in the history of your nation or people group? Has God completed his purposes for the group to which you belong?

6. Naomi was willing to let Ruth the Moabitess follow her back to her homeland. How did Ruth know that Naomi had accepted her? Are we willing to take "foreigners" with us as we go on with our lives and ministries? Discuss how these other groups of people will know if you and the church where you worship have accepted them.

Be prepared to discuss these questions and any other questions or issues that come to mind when your instructor refers to them in class.

CHAPTER 6

The Pattern of God's Mission in the Poetical Books

*T*he kingdom of priests is a foundational understanding in this section of the Bible. Life in the kingdom was blessed because life in the covenant kingdom was designed to have an impact on those who lived outside of it. Those who saw the blessings of God on His people would want to join the people of God (York, 41).

God's people celebrated this blessed life in songs and proverbs. They used these forms of poetry to remind each other of their place in the mission of God. The Psalms and the other poetical books celebrate the blessings of life in God's wonderful kingdom.

Missio Dei in Job

Job is the earliest of the books in the Wisdom Literature. The Wisdom Literature is made up of the artistic books of poetry, proverb, and lament. Since the understandings and feelings expressed in the Wisdom Literature are inspired by God, they present a godly point of view on all major areas of life. Their timeless wisdom remains useful for us today.

The books of Wisdom Literature do not typically tell stories and they are not primarily prophecies. However, they are inspired and accurate and they reveal much about what was to come in the *Missio Dei*. They show how life in God's wonderful kingdom is better than life outside of it. This "better life" inside of God's kingdom is displayed so that other nations are irresistibly drawn to join in this wise and blessed covenant relationship with God! The events in the book of Job probably occurred before Israel became a nation. The fact that Job does not refer to Moses or the Law that Moses wrote perhaps may indicate that it was written before the time of Moses. Job probably lived before there was a Jewish nation! If this is true, then we see that by including Job in the Bible, God has shown an illustration of how He cares for people of all nations.

> *The Creator was concerned about all races of people.*

The fact that God was close to Job and his family indicates that the Creator was concerned about all races of people long before the time of Israel. God held Job and his family accountable for their actions. In fact, He even gave Job a clear understanding of the resurrection:

> *Oh, that my words were recorded,*
> *that they were written on a scroll,*
> *that they were inscribed with an iron tool on lead,*
> *or engraved in rock forever!*
>
> *I know that my Redeemer lives,*
> *and that in the end He will stand upon the earth.*
>
> *And after my skin has been destroyed,*
> *yet in my flesh I will see God;*
> *I myself will see Him with my own eyes —*
> *I, and not another.*
>
> *How my heart yearns within me!*
> *(Job 19:23-27).*

Think of the revealed truths God shared with Job: the need for an enduring revelation "written on a scroll;" the awareness that God will come to redeem His people; the certainty of a personal, conscious resurrection after death; and the inner longing for our eternal home with God. All of this was given to someone outside the family of the Jews before they even existed. Surely God cares for all the nations!

Job's story is remarkable because of the intense suffering he went through without knowing why. Although Job never stopped believing in God, he questioned many things that God did and wanted to defend himself to God. Although God finally responded to Job, He did not give him a list of reasons for his sufferings. Instead, He gave him an overwhelming revelation of His glory and wisdom:

> *Then Job replied to the Lord:*
> *"I know that you can do all things;*
> *no plan of yours can be thwarted.*
> *You asked,*
> *'Who is this that obscures my counsel without knowledge?'*
> *Surely I spoke of things I did not understand,*
> *things too wonderful for me to know…*
> *My ears had heard of you*
> *but now my eyes have seen you.*
> *Therefore I…repent in dust and ashes"*
> *(Job 42:1-3, 5, 6b).*

Job's repentance led to the greatest blessings of his life, and also a personal encounter with God. We must do the same when God visits us.

When faced with difficulty, we do not always understand what is happening. Still, God's mission will not be defeated: *No plan of yours can be thwarted"* (v. 2). God's plan to bless all nations will certainly prevail!

Missio Dei in the Psalms

The book of Psalms is the songbook of Israel. The Jews used music in their worship, and the words of their songs were poetry. Jewish poetry did not have rhyme or meter; instead, it often used parallel thoughts.

One line would state a truth, and the second line would state a similar thought or restate the same thought in a different way. Together, the parallel thoughts made the point more clear and memorable. In Psalm 2, when the Father speaks to the Son, His words are an example of Hebrew parallelism.

> *Ask of me,*
> *and I will make the nations your inheritance,*
> *the ends of the earth your possession*
> *(Psalm 2:8).*

The second and third lines are parallel ideas. The thought of "nations" is further explained in the parallel thought "ends of the earth." An "inheritance" is also a "possession." The repetition emphasizes the idea and helps us to remember the lesson. Notice that "the nations" are the inheritance that God the Father promised to give to His Son in this Hebrew song!

The Universal Rule of God

The Hebrew songbook was written by Israelites who read the Pentateuch. They were aware of the promised blessing for all nations in the books of Moses. A key theme in the Psalms is the universal rule of God. By "universal," we mean that God's rule applies to all places and all people. The King who is celebrated in the Psalms is not willing to be served by only some of the nations because the scope of the kingdom is important to the King!

The presence of this theme in the Psalms also shows us that their human authors and many of the Israelites had a universal vision. They understood that the Pentateuch taught about a blessing-plan of God that included all nations.

The scope of the kingdom is important to the King!

New Testament believers urgently need a universal vision as well. Now that we have the gospel, we cannot afford to have less vision than the Old Testament people of Israel showed in their songs.

The words that describe the nations are everywhere in the Psalms. If you underline God's concern for the nations with a colored marker, the book will change colors before your eyes! Look at the examples in Figure 6.1 taken from Psalms 94-105:

Psalm	Quotation
Ps 94:10	Does he who disciplines **nations** not punish?
Ps 95:3	For the Lord is...the great **King above all** gods
Ps 96:3	Declare His Glory among the **nations**, his marvelous deeds among **all peoples.**
Ps 97:1	The Lord reigns, let **the earth** be glad; let the **distant shores** rejoice.
Ps 98:3	...all the **ends of the earth** have seen the salvation of our God.
Ps 99:2	... he is exalted over **all the nations.**
Ps 100:1	Shout for joy to the Lord, **all the earth.**
Ps 102:22	**...the peoples** and **the kingdoms** assemble to worship the Lord.
Ps 103:19	...his kingdom rules over **all.**
Ps 105:1	...make known **among the nations** what he has done.

Figure 6.1

Sometimes the repetition of this theme is so frequent that it almost shouts to us to share God's concern for all the nations! However, not every Christian has noticed the message.

> *More than forty Psalms deal with the topic of the salvation of the nations.*

Most Christians who read the Psalms say that they are about the troubles we face in life and how God helps us in them. While the Psalms do discuss how God helps us in our troubles, to miss the *Missio Dei* in the Psalms is to read them blindly. The nations, the peoples, the ends of the earth, the nobles of the nations, the coastlands, the distant shores — all of these are found in the Psalms, and more.

Like Joshua, many Israelites meditated on the Word of God. We are blessed to have the Bible to read and reflect upon. The Psalms are a wonderful place to spend time in prayerful reading. You will find God's mission there!

More than forty Psalms deal with the topic of the salvation of the nations. These psalms make a good study when you read them daily for several weeks. Try reading one *"Missio Dei"* Psalm a day for six weeks. Or, for a more focused study, read six Psalms a day for one week. Mark the Psalms as you read them in the boxes below in Figure 6.2. You should also mark the key lines about the *Missio Dei* that you discover in your Bible.

Meditating on the *Missio Dei* in the Psalms						
Sun	**Mon**	**Tues**	**Wed**	**Thurs**	**Fri**	**Sat**
Psalm 2	9	18	22	33	45	46
47	48	49	57	65	67	68
72	76	77	79	82	83	86
87	94	95	96	97	98	99
100	102	103	105	108	114	117
118	126, 138	139	144	145	146	150

Figure 6.2

If you want to do further Bible study or prepare a sermon on the topic, you could also write down the answers to the following questions:

- How does this Psalm refer to the nations that God loves?
- What does the Psalm call the nations to do?
- Do we as believers obey the instructions of this Psalm?
- Are we as believers helping other people or nations to obey this Psalm?

As you teach and preach from the Psalms, be sure to tell the people how these wonderful songs remind us that our God is King over all the earth.

We should celebrate His universal rule in our worship. We also should pray about how we may advance His kingdom to other people groups around the world!

The Royal Son Who Inherits the Nations — Psalm 2

Some of the Psalms specifically celebrate the royal kings of Israel. One example is Psalm 2:

> *"I have installed my King*
> *on Zion, my holy hill."*
> *I will proclaim the decree of the Lord:*
> *He said to me, 'You are My Son, today I have become your Father.*
> *Ask of me, and I will make the nations your inheritance...'*
> *Therefore, you kings, be wise;*
> *be warned, you rulers of the earth.*
> *Serve the Lord with fear and rejoice with trembling.*
> *Kiss the Son, lest He be angry...*
> *Blessed are all who take refuge in him*
> *(Psalm 2:6-8a, 10-12a, 12c).*

In this Psalm, the Jews are celebrating a coronation. A historical prince or "royal son" is being crowned king, and the words used are very powerful. They seem to go beyond simply describing King David or one of his descendants. In fact, they are describing a greater King, as well; a King before whom all the rulers of the earth will tremble. Although the rulers will serve Him with fear, He is also a King who blesses all who come to take refuge in His kingdom!

How can we understand this powerful language? This song is not only about David's family but also about the Messiah. The Royal Psalms are also Messianic Psalms, and the King they describe is the great Son of David, the Messiah. His rule will one day be fully recognized by all the other kings and peoples of the earth.

In Acts 13, Paul quotes this Royal Messianic Psalm in one of his missionary sermons:

> *We tell you the good news:*
> *What God promised our fathers he has fulfilled for us, their children,*
> *by raising up Jesus.*
> *As it is written in the second Psalm:*
> **'You are My Son; today I have become your Father.'**
> *…Therefore, my brothers, I want you to know that*
> **through Jesus the forgiveness of sins is proclaimed to you**
> *(Acts 13:32-33, 3; emphasis mine).*

King Jesus was crowned by His Father as the royal Son of God Who came to bring salvation to anyone who will accept His rule! This was the content of Paul's missionary message.

Jesus' resurrection is a powerful sign of His ability to bless those who take refuge in Him. How marvelous to preach the message of the coronation of the King to a lost world!

Connecting the Covenants — Psalm 47

God's covenants with Abraham and David are at the core of His relationship with His people. As Israelites worshipped God, they would be certain to sing about the covenants and their meaning. Is there evidence of this connection in the Psalms?

For an answer, look carefully at the three sections of Psalm 47, beginning with verses 1-4:

> *Clap your hands, all you nations;*
> *shout to God with cries of joy.*
> *How awesome is the Lord Most High,*
> *The great King over all the earth!*
> *He subdued nations under us,*
> *peoples under our feet.*
> *He chose our inheritance for us,*
> *the pride of Jacob, whom he loved*
> *(Psalm 47:1-4).*

These are kingdom words that remind us of David's "forever covenant." God is the King of all the earth Who provided Israelites with their inheritance. He has the authority and power to rule. Now look at verses 5-6:

> *God has ascended amid shouts of joy,*
> *the Lord amid the sounding of trumpets.*
> *Sing praises to God, sing praises;*
> *sing praises to our King, sing praises.*
> *For God is the King of all the earth;*
> *sing to Him a psalm of praise*
> *(Psalm 47:5-6).*

This section of the Psalms also sounds familiar because it is a coronation psalm, like Psalm 2. The great King (the Messiah) is ascending up to His throne as trumpets sound and His people sing His praise. These first six verses remind us of God's choice of King David and of the wonderful "forever kingdom" God promised to him. The kingdom is eternal because God is on the throne! Clearly, the Davidic Covenant is found in the Psalms.

One may question, "How does all this relate to the earlier covenant promises given to Abraham? Is the Abrahamic Covenant to bless all nations found in the Psalms as well?" For the answers to these questions, read verses 8 and 9 of the Psalm:

> *God reigns over the nations;*
> *God is seated on his holy throne.*
> **The nobles of the nations assemble**
> **as the people of the God of Abraham,**
> *for the kings of the earth belong to God;*
> *he is greatly exalted*
> *(Psalm 47:8-9; emphasis mine).*

The beginning phrase of verse 9 (highlighted above) is one of the most dramatic lines in the Psalms. *"The nobles of the nations assemble as the people of the God of Abraham."* Imagine the scene described in this Psalm:

The Psalm shows us the coronation of the great King. The Israelites are praising the God who gave them the covenants. Songs are sung and shouts are raised as God steps up to His holy throne.

Now, as we continue looking, we see coming the kings and leaders of all the nations! They are gathered together before God in unity. They have not come to the United Nations, but to the King of the nations. They are the people of the God of Abraham! There they stand before the throne with Abraham, blessed in the presence of the King.

Here in Psalm 47, the hope for the world is not in human effort, but in the blessing of God promised to Abraham so long ago. All nations are saying, "We joyfully accept our place in the covenant people. We have come to attend His coronation. We are the ones God promised to bless through Abraham!"

The appearance of Abraham and his covenant promises at the coronation celebration of the great King is significant. The covenant with David (eternal kingdom) is now joined to the covenant with Abraham (blessing for all nations). The connection is made.

God rules over all the earth in an eternal kingdom (David) — and all the earth is blessed as He fulfills His promises (Abraham). Hallelujah!

Prayer #5

Almighty Father, I worship you.
I am not a Jew.
If membership in Your kingdom depended on my race,
I would not have been included.
I was a Gentile sinner, without hope and without God in the world —
but You remembered me!
You saved me by the power of the cross.
Today I am one of God's people, a member of the family of God.
Thank You for including me!
Thank You for raising up Abraham's family
so that I also could be blessed.
Thank You for raising up David's kingdom
so that I also could have a King.
Holy Spirit, remind me of the nations that are still waiting today
to hear this good news.
In King Jesus' name I pray,
Amen!

Figure 6.3

The Purpose of God's Blessings — Psalm 67

Other Psalms also build on the earlier teachings in the Pentateuch. Psalm 67 takes words of the blessing that Aaron the high priest used for blessing the Israelites (Numbers 6:24-26). The Psalm then connects these words with Israel's role to be a kingdom of priests to all nations:

> *May God be gracious to us*
> *and bless us*
> *and make his face shine upon us...*
> *(Psalm 67:1).*

Up to this point, the words of this Psalm reflect the basic concerns of mankind everywhere. They could be spoken by the followers of many religions. Sadly, this is both the first and last point in the theology of many Christians. "May God bless me" is the beginning and ending of many Christian prayers. We can do better, and Psalm 67 shows us how.

God does bless His people in wonderful ways. However, the great joy in serving God is not just that He blesses us, but that He will also make us a blessing to others. This is the same thing that God promised Abraham in Genesis 12:2. The key point of Psalm 67 is not in the first line, *"May God... bless us,"* but in the second:

> *...that your ways may be known on earth,*
> *your salvation among all nations*
> *(Psalm 67:2).*

This verse shows us the reason for blessings from God. They are given so that we may be effective in being a blessing to others! Life in the kingdom does not have an inward focus. The purpose of God's people aims outward towards the nations that He loves.

Indeed, do bless us, God — so that we may have the strength and provisions to make Your ways known on earth! Do let Your face shine on us with blessings — so that we may reflect the light of Your blessed salvation to the nations!

This wonderful lesson from verses one and two is repeated in the last two verses of the Psalm as well:

> *Then the land will yield its harvest,*
> *and God, our God, will bless us.*
> *God will bless us,*
> *and all the ends of the earth will fear him.*
> *(Psalm 67:6-7).*

So the purpose for God's blessings is explained twice, both at the beginning and end of the Psalm. The lesson is balanced at the beginning and end of the song.

The verses arranged just inside the lesson are exact copies of each other. They are prayers of petition that call for God to receive the worship of all people groups on earth:

> *May the peoples praise you, O God:*
> *may all the peoples praise you...*
>
> *...May the peoples praise you, O God:*
> *may all the peoples praise you*
> *(Psalm 67:3, 5).*

In the exact middle of the song comes the truth upon which all of these lessons and prayers are balancing: the universal scope of the kingdom of God!

> *May the nations be glad and sing for joy,*
> *for you rule the peoples justly*
> *and guide the nations of the earth*
> *(Psalm 67:4).*

Israelites were to use their blessings to attract the nations to God.

To summarize, the central truth of Psalm 67 is the universal kingdom of God. The repeated prayer was to see all the nations praise Him. The lesson learned was that the Israelites must use their blessings to attract the nations to God's kingdom. God, who is the rightful King, will not receive the worship that belongs to Him until we use our blessings correctly.

Small Psalm, Big Message — Psalm 117

Even the shortest Psalm in the songbook has room to celebrate the *Missio Dei*. In it the nations (Gentiles) are commanded to praise Yahweh, the covenant God of Israel:

> *Praise the **Lord**, all you **nations**;*
> *extol Him, all you peoples.*
> *For great is his love toward us,*
> *and the faithfulness of the Lord endures forever.*
> *Praise the Lord*
> *(Psalm 117:1-2; emphasis mine).*

The word translated *Lord* is *Yahweh*, the name used in the Old Testament for Israel's covenant God. The word for *nations* is *goyim*, which means the Gentiles. Psalm 117 is calling on the *Gentile nations* to join in the worship of Israel's *covenant God!*

The God of the Bible is a missionary God, and the Israelites were God's missionary people. The Israelites were frequently reminded of their calling when they worshipped because they often sang missionary songs. Christians today also need to be surrounded with truths in their teaching and worship that remind them of our calling to the nations!

Missio Dei in the Wisdom of Solomon

The son who took David's place on the throne was Solomon. King Solomon built the temple of the Lord in Jerusalem. Solomon's prayer of dedication for the new temple is found in 1 Kings 8 and 2 Chronicles 6. Although not every scholar agrees, most conservative scholars believe that Solomon wrote Ecclesiastes, the Song of Songs, and most of the book of Proverbs.

Success and Failure in the Life of Solomon

Solomon's life is an interesting contrast. He started his career very well as he prayed for wisdom to rule Israel. God was pleased with this request (1 Kings 3). God gave Solomon more talent and intellectual ability than any other person alive in his generation (1 Kings 4:29-34). His kingdom also grew and became very famous and wealthy.

When Solomon prayed his prayer of dedication for the temple, he showed an excellent knowledge of theology:

> *O Lord, God of Israel,*
> *there is no God like You in heaven above or on earth below —*
> *you who keep your covenant of love with your servants*
> *who continue wholeheartedly in your way…*
>
> *Now Lord, God of Israel,*
> *keep for your servant David my father the promises you made to Him when*
> *you said,*
> *'You shall never fail to have a man to sit before me on the throne of Israel,*
> *if only your sons are careful in all they do to walk before me as you have done.'*
>
> *…But will God really dwell on earth?*
> *The heavens, even the highest heaven, cannot contain you.*
> *How much less this temple I have built!*
> *(1 Kings 8:23, 25, 27).*

Solomon was well aware of God's kingdom promises to David. He also knew of God's covenant promises to bless the nations:

> *As for the foreigner who does not belong to your people Israel*
> *but has come from a distant land because of your name —*
> *for men will hear of your great name*
> *and your mighty hand and your outstretched arm —*
> *when he comes and prays toward this temple,*
> *then hear from heaven, your dwelling place,*
> *and do whatever the foreigner asks of you,*
> *so that all the peoples of the earth may know your name and fear you,*
> *as do your own people Israel…*
> *(1 Kings 8:41-43b).*

Solomon's prayer for the foreigners is a clear example of the purpose of the Israelite nation. Israelites knew that they were blessed to bring God's blessings to all nations.

Israel Ministers to the Nation of Sheba

A good example of Solomon's early success was the visit of the Queen of Sheba. This queen traveled from Africa (or possibly southern Arabia) to Jerusalem to investigate the wisdom and success of Solomon.

> *When the queen of Sheba heard about the fame of Solomon*
> *and his relation to the name of the Lord,*
> *she came to test him with hard questions...*
>
> *When the queen of Sheba saw all the wisdom of Solomon*
> *and the palace he had built...*
> *and the burnt offerings he made at the temple of the Lord,*
> *she was overwhelmed.*
> *She said to the king, "The report I heard in my own country*
> *about your achievements and your wisdom is true...*
> *How happy your men must be!*
> *How happy your officials,*
> *who continually stand before you and hear your wisdom!"*
> *(1 Kings 10:1, 4, 5b-6, 8).*

Notice how the Queen of Sheba, who was not an Israelite, was blessed by what she saw when she visited the people of God. Overwhelmed by God's goodness, she cried out: "how happy your men must be!" This is an example of how the good life inside the covenant Kingdom of God could attract people of other nations to the one true God.

> *"Praise be to the Lord your God,*
> *who has delighted in you and placed you on the throne of Israel.*
> *Because of the Lord's eternal love for Israel, he has made you king,*
> *to maintain justice and righteousness"*
> *...Then she left and returned with her retinue to her own country.*
> *(I Kings 10:9, 13b).*

The analysis of the queen of Sheba was that Israel's God made Israel a blessed place. Her visit to Israel gave her new understanding of the character of the one true God. She learned about God's covenants and kingdom and returned to her homeland with new insights. She could appreciate the blessings and wisdom of the Kingdom of God. On this occasion, the people of Israel served their purpose as a kingdom of priests for the nation of Sheba!

Solomon Chooses Sin instead of the Covenant Blessings

Although Solomon surpassed all others in riches and fame, wealth and success seem to have ruined him. He forgot the purposes of his blessings (see commentary on Psalm 67), and later in life his desires spoiled his wisdom. Unfortunately, Solomon married many foreign wives for political and personal reasons, and these wives turned his heart toward foreign gods (1 Kings 11:4).

To please his new wives, Solomon allowed them to keep their foreign religions. He also built places of worship for Ashtoreth, goddess of Sidon, and for Molech, the god of Ammon (1 Kings 11:1-8).

The worship of false gods that Solomon introduced to Israel would plague the kingdom for centuries. The worship of Ashtoreth celebrated sexual immorality, and the worship of Molech involved sacrificing children in fire. Eventually these wicked religions destroyed the kingdoms of Israel and Judah.

God's judgment on Solomon's sins was to remove the northern ten tribes from his kingdom (1 Kings 11:9-13). The northern ten tribes became *Israel*. The southern tribes ruled by Solomon's descendants were known as *Judah*. As in the days of Babel, God divided the people to delay them from uniting against Him.

At a happier time of his life, Solomon wrote the following proverb:

> *Above all else, guard your heart, for it is the wellspring of life*
> *(Proverbs 4:23).*

If only King Solomon had remained true to the way of wisdom and followed his own good advice! Then Israelites could have been kept from sin and continued to bless the nations around them.

The Bible does not explain all the reasons for Solomon's fall. Perhaps he became ill or depressed and acted out of his ordinary character. Perhaps he lived with chronic pain and became bitter, or he may have become proud. Perhaps he simply gave in to temptation. We have no record that he ever repented or gained victory over his struggles. How much misery would have been avoided if Solomon had stayed true to God!

Lessons from the Life of Solomon

Solomon's life is a good reminder to us that we should always be accountable to other people. As Christian leaders, each one of us needs to have godly brothers and sisters who will challenge us if we begin to sin. We must not depend on our talents or achievements, for these will not impress God at the judgment. God is looking at our hearts.

Our blindness to our own sins is a terrible problem. For this reason, God sends us His Holy Spirit to convict us. Conviction is painful, but it can save our lives!

Conviction is painful, but it can save our lives!

> *Our fathers disciplined us for a little while as they thought best;*
> *but God disciplines us for our good, that we may share in his holiness.*
> *No discipline seems pleasant at the time, but painful.*
> *Later on, however, it produces a harvest of righteousness and peace*
> *for those who have been trained by it*
> *(Hebrews 12:10-11).*

The Holy Spirit is also able to comfort and counsel us. If someone as talented as Solomon could fail, then all of us must also be on our guard. Solomon's life is a reminder of our need for the ministry of the Holy Spirit!

> *Unless I go away, the Counselor will not come to you;*
> *but if I go, I will send him to you.*
> *When he comes, he will convict the world of guilt*
> *in regard to sin and righteousness and judgment…*
> *when he, the Spirit of Truth, comes,*
> *he will guide you into all truth*
> *(John 16:7b-8, 13a).*

How blessed you are if you have caring and honest friends who are used by the Holy Spirit to keep you accountable. No one is so gifted or important that he or she can stand alone. Success without humility can be more deadly than failure in the end.

Proverbs: The Blessed Life in the Kingdom

Most of the book of Proverbs seems to have been written by Solomon in the earlier part of his life. These proverbs contain much wisdom and do not seem as cynical as his later writings.

A proverb is a short, memorable statement that explains the way of wisdom to anyone who will listen. A proverb uses word pictures or metaphors to create vivid illustrations of timeless truth. These vivid words make the lesson hard to forget.

Biblical proverbs are inspired by God. The proverbs were a tool that the Israelites used in their work as a kingdom of priests to the nations. Proverbs were commonly used in the kingdoms and cultures that surrounded Israel. By explaining the wisdom of the Kingdom of God in proverbs, Israelites could communicate truth about God to other nations.

When they heard Israel's proverbs, the nations could see that life in the Kingdom of God was blessed life because God's principles work. If you live your life by God's wisdom, you will be blessed:

> *The fear of the Lord is the beginning of knowledge,*
> *but fools despise wisdom and discipline*
> *(Proverbs 1:7).*

The proverbs share God's kingdom wisdom on very practical issues. When the people of the nations observed God's enlightened principles, they were drawn to participate in His kingdom (see Proverbs 1:7; 2:6-8; and 3:5-6).

To outsiders looking in, God's nation of Israel was blessed. People were attracted to Israel's God when they heard Israel's wisdom! Proverbs were written that covered many aspects of life. Notice the variety of topics included in the wise proverbs listed in Figures 6.4, 6.5, and 6.6.

Proverbs Concerning How to Govern Well
Righteousness exalts a nation, *but sin is a disgrace to any people. (Proverbs 14:34)*
Acquitting the guilty and condemning the innocent — *the Lord detests them both. (Proverbs 17:15)*
By justice a king gives a country stability, *but one who is greedy for bribes tears it down. (Proverbs 29:4)*

Figure 6.4

If the king of Israel read these proverbs and lived by them, his people would be blessed. These principles will work in any nation!

Proverbs Giving Kingdom Principles for Businessmen
Honest scales and balances are from the Lord; *all the weights in the bag are of his making. (Proverbs 16:11)*
The plans of the diligent lead to profit *As surely as haste leads to poverty. (Proverbs 21:5)*
A fortune made by a lying tongue *is a fleeting vapor and a deadly snare. (Proverbs 21:6)*

Figure 6.5

God's Word is practical enough to give help to businessmen and businesswomen. A business that applies God's wisdom is prepared to prosper more than a business operated by other guidelines. Honesty, diligence, and truthfulness are some of God's keys to success in our working lives.

Proverbs Showing God's Wisdom for Marriage and Family
Drink water from your own cistern, running water from your own well... *May your fountain be blessed, and may you rejoice in the wife of your* *youth. (Proverbs 5:15, 18)*
Discipline your son, for in that there is hope; *do not be a willing party to his death. (Proverbs 19:18)*
The righteous man leads a blameless life; *blessed are his children after him. (Proverbs 20:7)*

Figure 6.6

Even marriage and family are included in the wise advice of the Proverbs. God recommends sexual purity, attention to children, and righteous living as keys to having a successful marriage and a healthy family.

The Proverbs spoke the message of wisdom to anyone who would listen. They invited others to participate in the blessing of kingdom living. These proverbs were a practical and cultural way of expressing God's truth. They reached new generations of Jews and also attracted the surrounding nations that were the focus of the *Missio Dei*.

Song of Songs: Human Sexuality under God's Covenant

Another of King Solomon's earlier writings was the Song of Songs (sometimes called the Song of Solomon). This book celebrates the strength and beauty of married love between a man and woman who live under God's covenant together. Emotional and physical love in the safe boundaries of marriage is not shameful or unmentionable! In fact, it is celebrated:

> *Place me like a seal over your heart,*
> *like a seal on your arm;*
> *for love is as strong as death…*
> *Many waters cannot quench love;*
> *rivers cannot wash it away.*
> *If one were to give all the wealth of his house for love,*
> *it would be utterly scorned*
> *(Song of Songs 8:6a, 7).*

Song of Songs shows that marriage relationships in the covenant are superior to the so-called *love* of the idolatrous religions. The *love* discussed in the sinful world is often nothing more than immorality and selfish lust. It does not truly satisfy the woman or the man; instead, it harms them both emotionally, and it can be physically destructive as well.

Diseases such as HIV/AIDS and syphilis would become non-existent if people limited their sexuality to the marriage partner alone. In fact, God's plan for sexual morality could stop the AIDS pandemic in one generation.

In addition, immoral sexuality is often accompanied by violence. This may be violence done by forcing someone to have sex, or violence committed afterward by someone offended by the act of immorality. God says not to wrong another person in this way.

Men and women damaged by immoral sexuality have a harder time experiencing a godly marriage or raising a godly family. They are in danger of losing their capacity for joy and fruitfulness. They may also lose their testimony, or even their lives. God knows this. He wants us to be blessed; so He warns us of the terrible dangers associated with the sin of sexual immorality.

Immoral sexuality has a destructive effect on both men and women. That is why sexual immorality is detestable to God. However, there is a wholesome sexuality that occurs between one man and his wife in covenant in relationship under God.

Marriage partners have made a promise covenant to God and to each other to be trustworthy. Since they desire to honor God and to bless each another, their sexual love belongs exclusively and absolutely to one another. This means that they share their sexual love *only* with one another, and they share *all* of it with one another! No other person can ever enter that sacred space, as the Song of Songs shows us: "You are a garden locked up, my sister, my bride; you are a spring enclosed, a sealed fountain" (Song of Songs 4:12).

It must be stated strongly that this requirement of sexual purity does not apply only to the woman. The biblical responsibility to remain sexually pure rests equally on the man and the woman. It is ungodly, self-righteous bigotry for men to live sexually immoral lives while requiring their wives to be sexually pure. While some religions allow this kind of distinction, biblical Christianity does not.

An unequal requirement of virginity for only one of the partners completely destroys the beauty and potential of the future marriage. No man who lives like this will ever experience a blessed marriage, regardless of his race or religion. He will be most severely judged by God. In fact, the prophet Malachi says that God will not accept such a man's prayers — unless he repents!

> *You flood the Lord's altar with tears.*
> *You weep and wail because he no longer pays attention to your offerings*
> *or accepts them with pleasure from your hands.*
> *You ask, "Why?"*
> *It is because the Lord is acting as the witness*
> *between you and the wife of your youth,*
> *because you have broken faith with her,*
> *though she is your partner, the wife of your marriage covenant*
> *(Malachi 2:13-14).*

Children of a godly, covenant marriage are more likely to display God's glory and wisdom.

Immoral sexuality will be judged. God hates it because it is destructive, sinful, and selfish. He commands each of us to guard his or her own spirit (see also Proverbs 4:23). God will not overlook sexual sins, divorce, or violence done against the woman in marriage. If a man and woman want to serve God, their marriage must follow God's covenant requirements!

However, the sexuality of a man and wife given exclusively to each other under God's covenant is not sinful. Such a relationship requires an absolutely tender attitude of care for one another that God can bless. This kind of love leads to a sexual relationship that does not harm the woman or the man. It produces godly affection that holds the marriage together for a lifetime. It also produces godly children that God can love and use (read Malachi 2:15).

Any healthy couple can produce children, but to produce godly children is a greater challenge! Godly children are less likely to come from an ungodly marriage. However, the pure covenant love of a man and woman under God can create a stable environment to raise children that serve the Lord.

Children of a godly, covenant marriage are likely to display God's glory and wisdom, and such children are secure. They feel loved and they can learn to love God and love others. A covenant marriage and the children it produces can cause the light of God's covenant to shine brightly in the world!

A godly marriage is a great testimony to the nations of the power of God. If God can enter the most sensitive, personal areas of life and cause them to shine for His glory, then the nations will see and know that He is God.

Ecclesiastes: The Need for Completed Revelation

Most scholars believe that Solomon wrote the book of Ecclesiastes and that he wrote it late in his life. If they are correct, then this book shows a contrast between two aspects of Solomon's mind. On one hand, he had become cynical and he feared that life was meaningless. On the other hand, he indicated that the fear of the Lord was still significant in his life.

> *The words of the Teacher, son of David, king in Jerusalem:*
> *"Meaningless! Meaningless!" says the Teacher.*
> *"Utterly meaningless! Everything is meaningless"*
> *(Ecclesiastes 1:1-2).*

Solomon knew many things, but he needed a further revelation from God. He did not have access to the later prophetic writings or the New Testament. He needed the completed revelation of God — the full Bible. Solomon was missing something that we are blessed to have!

> *Remember your Creator in the days of your youth,*
> *before the days of trouble come*
> *and the years approach when you will say,*
> *"I find no pleasure in them"*
> *(Ecclesiastes 12:1).*

No Satisfaction apart from God's Word

Solomon, who was impressively educated and very intelligent, did not find wise answers for the questions that bothered him. He needed to hear something more from God. Unfortunately, his sins kept him from hearing what God was saying. Neither knowledge nor pleasure could satisfy his soul:

> *For with much wisdom comes much sorrow;*
> *the more knowledge, the more grief.*
> *I thought in my heart,*
> *"Come now, I will test you with pleasure to find out what is good."*
> *But that also proved to be meaningless.*
> *"Laughter," I said, "is foolish.*
> *And what does pleasure accomplish?"*
> *(Ecclesiastes 1:18-2:2).*

Observing the failure of knowledge and pleasure to fill his emptiness, Solomon turned to power, fame, and achievement. Perhaps these held the key to the meaning of life:

> *I undertook great projects:*
> *I built houses for myself and planted vineyards.*
> *I made gardens and parks and planted all kinds of fruit trees in them.*
> *I made reservoirs to water groves of flourishing trees.*
> *I bought male and female slaves...*
> *Yet when I surveyed all that my hands had done*
> *and what I had toiled to achieve,*
> *everything was meaningless, a chasing after the wind;*
> *nothing was gained under the sun"*
> *(Ecclesiastes 2:4-7a, 11).*

Great achievement and absolute power did nothing to answer his questions. Solomon was troubled by an ultimate question: what is the future of the soul of man? Since our lives are so short, we struggle against death and call out for more time to live. Solomon did not understand eternal life with God after death; so the injustice of both life and death drove him to a dark depression!

> *So I reflected on all this*
> *and concluded that the righteous and the wise and what they do*
> *are in God's hands,*
> *but no man knows whether love or hate awaits him.*
> *All share a common destiny —*
> *the righteous and the wicked, the good and the bad...*

> *This is the evil in everything that happens under the sun:*
> *The same destiny overtakes all.*
> *The hearts of men, moreover, are full of evil*
> *and there is madness in their hearts while they live,*
> *and afterward they join the dead*
> *(Ecclesiastes 9:1-2a, 3).*

Solomon needed to know about heaven! He also needed a significant mission for his life on earth; he needed to remember the *Missio Dei*. Somehow, he had forgotten it. His sins undoubtedly kept him from hearing God clearly. Yet at the end of his life, he was still clutching to a faint memory of the God who will judge all at the last day. He knew that serving God was the heart of life, but he had forgotten how.

> *Now all has been heard;*
> *here is the conclusion of the matter:*
> *Fear God and keep his commandments,*
> *for this is the whole duty of man.*
> *For God will bring every deed into judgment,*
> *including every hidden thing,*
> *whether it is good or evil*
> *(Ecclesiastes 12:13-14).*

Practical Lessons from Solomon's Life

What a peril awaits those in the Kingdom of God who forget the purpose of their existence! No earthly pursuit can satisfy the Christian other than the pursuit of God and His mission. We were made for another world and this world's pursuits will never satisfy us. We cannot be happy if we forget our purpose.

Around the world there are many Christians who do not know why

Around the world there are many Christians who do not know why they exist. How can we wake them from their slumber?

they exist. They have never been told of the mission of God. Perhaps they have fallen into one of the meaningless pursuits that consumed Solomon's life. How can we wake them from their slumber? How can we avoid the sad, selfish end of covenant people who forget the mission of God?

We have a completed Bible to read, which Solomon did not. God's completed revelation is a tremendous treasure. For instance, we know that there is a difference between the end of the godly and ungodly, which Jesus revealed to us:

> *When the Son of Man comes in his glory, and all the angels with him,*
> *he will sit on his throne in heavenly glory.*
> *All the nations will be gathered before him,*
> *and he will separate the people one from another*
> *as a shepherd separates the sheep from the goats.*
> *He will put the sheep on his right and the goats on his left.*
> *Then the King will say to those on his right,*
> *"Come, you who are blessed by my Father;*
> *take your inheritance,*
> *the kingdom prepared for you since the creation of the world."*
>
> *...Then he will say to those on his left,*
> *"Depart from me, you who are cursed,*
> *into the eternal fire prepared for the devil and his angels"*
> *(Matthew 25:31-34, 41).*

We know that God will judge sinners, and we also know that God will reward those who seek Him. This means that we have a positive motivation to serve and obey God!

> *...because anyone who comes to him [God]*
> *must believe that he exists*
> *and that he rewards those who earnestly seek him*
> *(Hebrews 11:6b).*

We also know that God is on a mission that gives meaning to this life. In addition, we know that God is giving us a part to play in His great mission. What a sense of purpose and meaning our lives can have!

> *Again Jesus said, "Peace be with you!*
> *As the Father has sent me, I am sending you."*
> *And with that He breathed on them and said,*
> *"Receive the Holy Spirit"*
> *(John 20:21-22).*

Hallelujah! We need not suffer with the sin and depression that afflicted Solomon. God gives us power in the Holy Spirit to live in holiness. We have significance in life, significance in mission, and significance in eternity. How wonderful is the door of service that God has opened up for us!

Prayer #6

Almighty God,
I will always be amazed
at how much You love me.
Remind me of the end of the godly!
Remind me of my purpose here on Earth!
Save me from intellect alone,
pleasure alone,
power alone,
achievement alone.
Keep me always as Your humble servant.
Help me find the meaning in my life
that only those who lose their lives for You can ever find.
Help me to wake up Your sleeping church
and joyfully enroll it in the wonderful mission of God!
In Jesus' precious Name I pray,
Amen!

Figure 6.7

Summary

The Wisdom Literature provided a cultural way of expressing truth to new generations of Jews and also to the surrounding nations that were the focus of the *Missio Dei*. The Proverbs spoke the message of wisdom to anyone who would listen. They invited others to participate in the blessing of kingdom living. Married love inside God's covenant is celebrated in the Song of Songs. It is attractive to people of any nation who see it because God's wisdom works in real life! Ecclesiastes teaches us that no earthly pursuit can satisfy the Christian other than the pursuit of God and His mission. We were made for another world, and we cannot be happy if we forget our purpose.

Review and Application

You have now completed your study of chapter 6 with its emphasis on the pattern of God's mission in the Poetical Books. Perhaps we should ask ourselves several related questions: "How will the wealth of information I've just studied affect my response to God's mission?" And, "Will I choose to incorporate some of this wealth of information on marital relationships into my counseling ministry?"

1. Explain the ultimate reason for the blessings God gives to His people, according to Psalm 67.

2. Why has God clearly commanded the people committed to His mission to abstain from sexual immorality?

3. Discuss the advantages that children born to a godly and loving Christian couple may have compared to children from non-believing families.

4. The text refers to "Christians who do not know why they exist." What do you think this means? Discuss your answers in the class.

5. What dangers can come to a church whose people forget their mission and focus on receiving blessings in this life?

Be prepared to discuss these questions and any other questions or issues that come to mind when your instructor refers to them in class.

Unit 3
The Realization of the Missio Dei

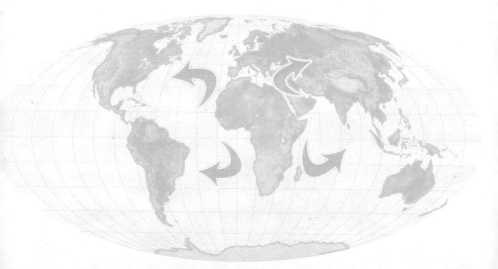

CHAPTER 7

The Messiah Foreseen in the Prophets

*T*he books from Isaiah to Malachi at the end of the Old Testament are called the Prophets. A prophet was someone who received a specific message from God to give to a person or group of people.

A prophet was not to prophesy unless God had given the message. Prophecy also was to contain the exact words God gave, not the words of the prophet himself. The prophet was to speak boldly, regardless of the people's response. People still need the ministry of prophecy today.

In the Old Testament, God gave His people kings to lead them and priests to teach them the Scriptures and the covenants of the Lord. The kings and priests served as a balance to each other, to keep each other from sinning and from misleading God's people. Yet even with this balanced arrangement, sometimes both the kings and priests would fail in their calling at the same time. Then they and the people would all become corrupt.

God used the prophets as a third powerful group of messengers to call kings, priests, and all His people back to their covenant relationship with Himself. God also used prophets to speak His message to the surrounding nations. The prophets were enforcement agents of the covenant and servants of the *Missio Dei!*

Covenant Lawsuit

God had made a covenant with the Israelites. They were to serve as a kingdom of priests for all the nations (Exodus 19:6). Their ministry and presence in the world was to make God famous and well desired among all nations. God was willing to bless Israel so greatly that the whole world would see and desire a similar relationship with Him.

However, Israelites had not fulfilled their part of the covenant. They had fallen into sins more wicked than those of the Canaanite nations they had replaced! They were not making God's name a blessing to the nations. Instead, the nations who dealt with Israel were blaspheming Israel's God because of the people's wicked behavior.

This could not be allowed to continue. In the prophetic books, God calls His people to account. After their sins were revealed and judgment was announced, God gave words of hope for the people who remained. God would allow a remnant to survive judgment and fulfill their place in God's mission.

God used the prophets symbolically to take His wayward people to court and make legal charges against them. They had accepted God's covenant blessings, but had failed to live by the covenant promises. In fact, they did not even care about the nations to whom they were intended to minister. God's honor among the nations was at stake! Ezekiel was one prophet who saw this clearly.

> *Therefore say to the house of Israel,*
> *"This is what the Sovereign Lord says…*
> *I will show the holiness of my great name,*
> *which has been profaned among the nations,*
> *the name you have profaned among them.*
> *Then the nations will know that I am the Lord"*
> *(Ezekiel 36:22-23a).*

God has a legal case against His people. The very ones who are supposed to love Him have broken His laws rebelliously. This is similar to what the apostle Paul would later write in the New Testament:

> *You who brag about the law, do you dishonor God by breaking the law?*
> *As it is written:*
> *"God's name is blasphemed among the Gentiles because of you"*
> *(Romans 2:23-24).*

What will God decide to do about the case against the nation of Israel? He sends His prophets to confront them as a lawyer or barrister would do in a court of law! He uses very powerful verbal images to confront and convict His sinful people.

A courtroom scene takes place in the book of Micah. God calls the mountains of Israel to serve as witnesses in the court:

> *Stand up, plead your case before the mountains;*
> *let the hills hear what you have to say.*
> *Hear, O mountains, the Lord's accusation;*
> *listen, you everlasting foundations of the earth.*
> *For the Lord has a case against his people;*
> *he is lodging a charge against Israel...*
> *(Micah 6:1-2).*

Sometimes the prophets are blamed for having a harsh message, but they had to speak strong words because of the people's stubborn sins. However, the prophets also spoke powerful words of hope and promise. They saw the day drawing near when the special offspring of the woman would crush Satan's head (Genesis 3:15). They gave instructions that would bring the people back into the blessed covenant with God:

> *He has showed you, O man, what is good.*
> *And what does the Lord require of you?*
> *To act justly*
> *and to love mercy*
> *and to walk humbly with your God*
> *(Micah 6:8).*

God Will Judge All Nations

Some people think that the prophets were sent only to Israel and Judah. However, this is not so. The prophets were also sent to hold other nations accountable for their own sins. God was the rightful ruler of the whole earth, not just Israel. The prophets knew that they were to speak to nations.

> *The word of the Lord came to me, saying,*
> *"Before I formed you in the womb I knew you,*
> *before you were born I set you apart;*
> *I appointed you as a prophet to the nations" (Jeremiah 1:4-5).*

We can see the *Missio Dei* in many places throughout the prophets. God often sent messages to nations outside of Israel. We see a powerful example of this in Jeremiah 25. No nation on earth is excluded from the message of God's prophet!

> *This is what the Lord, the God of Israel, said to me:*
> *"Take from my hand this cup filled with the wine of my wrath*
> *and make all the nations to whom I send you drink it."*
> ***...So I took the cup from the Lord's hand***
> ***and made all the nations to whom he sent me drink it:***
>
> *Jerusalem and the towns of Judah...*
> *Pharaoh king of Egypt... and all the foreign people there;*
> *all the kings of Uz;*
> *all the kings of the Philistines...*
> *Edom, Moab and Ammon;*
> *all the kings of Tyre and Sidon;*
> *the kings of the coastlands across the sea;*
> *Dedan, Tema, Buz and all who are in distant places;*
> *all the kings of Arabia and all the kings of the foreign people*
> *who live in the desert;*
> *all the kings of Zimri, Elam and Media;*
> *and all the kings of the north, near and far, one after the other —*
> ***all the kingdoms on the face of the earth...***
> *(Jeremiah 25:15, 17-18a, 19a-26a; emphasis mine).*

More than eighteen nations are included in this amazing list from the Old Testament. Certainly Jeremiah would have understood what Joshua had learned long ago: God is the Lord of All the Earth!

What was God's message to the nations? Jeremiah's prophecy continues:

> *Now prophesy all these words against them and say to them:*
> *"The Lord will roar from on high;*
> *he will thunder from His holy dwelling*
> *and roar mightily* **against his land.**
> *He will shout like those who tread the grapes,*
> *shout* **against all who live on the earth.**
> *The tumult will resound* **to the ends of the earth,**
> *for the Lord will bring charges* **against the nations;**
> *he will bring judgment* **on all mankind**
> *and put the wicked to the sword,"*
> *declares the Lord*
> *(Jeremiah 25:30-31; emphasis mine).*

God was not the God of the Jews only; He would roar in judgment against "His land" — the whole earth! He had the authority to rule all of it. All who broke His laws would have charges brought against them, for God will judge the sins of the wicked.

Some would complain that these are hard words; however, they must remember that these words would never have been spoken if the nations had not sinned against each other and against God.

These strong words are a great encouragement to anyone who has ever wondered why there does not seem to be justice on the earth. God sees the affairs of nations. No injustice can ever escape His notice because God is a just Judge. One day all nations will stand before God for judgment!

The New Covenant

One of the most significant revelations in the prophetic books concerns the New Covenant. The New Covenant spoken of by the prophet Jeremiah would be the basis of God's mission to the Gentiles.

> *"The time is coming," declares the Lord,*
> *"when I will make a new covenant with the house of Israel*
> *and with the house of Judah.*
> *It will not be like the covenant I made with their forefathers*
> *when I took them by the hand to lead them out of Egypt,*
> *because they broke my covenant, though I was a husband to them,"*
> *declares the Lord.*
> *"This is the covenant I will make with the house of Israel after that time,"*
> *declares the Lord.*
>
> *"I will put my law in their minds*
> *and write it on their hearts.*
> *I will be their God, and they will be my people...*
> *For I will forgive their wickedness*
> *and will remember their sins no more"*
> *(Jeremiah 31:31-33, 34b).*

God promised a new covenant whose requirements would be remembered, not forgotten. Moses' covenant was written on tablets of stone, but God's new covenant would be written on the minds and hearts of His people.

The new covenant would be a new demonstration of God's power to change people. Instead of rebelling, God's new people would be given power to remain faithful. How encouraging this message must have been to a weary prophet like Jeremiah!

God also said that in the new covenant He would forgive His people. He would provide a personal transformation that would make sinful people right with God again. The new covenant will center on God's final work of salvation, and this salvation will be for all the people groups of the world!

God's Mission of Blessing

The prophets often spoke of restoration that would occur after the time of judgment. Although disastrous punishment for sin must occur, God was not giving up on His work of redeeming lost humanity. He showed glimpses of the future to His servants, the prophets. God was about to win back the hearts of the peoples of the world.

The prophets spoke of a coming day when the nations would be among the redeemed. We have already seen how the Psalms sang repeatedly about the nations. The prophets continually spoke about the nations, too! It is useful to mark such prophecies in your study Bible.

Prophecies Dealing with the Salvation of the Nations

The prophets not only pronounced judgments but also called the nations to God's new work of salvation.

> *Turn to me and be saved, all you ends of the earth,*
> *for I am God, and there is no other*
> *(Isaiah 45:22).*

Salvation is sometimes referred to as God's "light for the nations." This imagery will be repeated in the New Testament.

> *The law will go out from me;*
> *my justice will become a light to the nations…*
> *My righteousness draws near speedily*
> *and my arm will bring justice to the nations*
> *(Isaiah 51:4-5).*

Not only are the nations called to the light of salvation, but it is also prophesied that they will in fact come and answer God's call! This type of prophecy is a prediction of the final victory of the *Missio Dei*.

> *The Lord will lay bare his holy arm in the sight of all the nations,*
> *and all the ends of the earth will see the salvation of our God*
> *(Isaiah 52:10).*

God's new program of salvation would cost a terrible price. No person could pay the cost of his or her own salvation. What a wonderful hope God offered the world through His servants the prophets! He would completely save everyone who comes to Him.

After salvation, new lives will need to be trained in the ways of the Lord. God provided for this need as well.

Prophecies Dealing with the Discipleship of the Nations

It is very interesting to discover some prophecies which revealed God's intent to make *disciples* of the international believers who would come to faith in the last days:

> *In the last days*
> *the mountain of the Lord's temple will be established*
> *as chief among the mountains;*
> *it will be raised above the hills,*
> *and peoples will stream to it.*
> *Many nations will come and say,*
> *"Come, let us go up to the mountain of the Lord,*
> *to the house of the God of Jacob.*
> *He will teach us his ways,*
> *so that we may walk in his paths"*
> *(Micah 4:1-2).*

Notice that the nations will freely choose to become disciples of the Lord. No one can become a disciple unless he or she wants to be discipled. Micah's wonderful vision shows us the people of the nations willingly coming to "the God of Jacob" so that they can learn to walk in His ways!

Many people reading this book are called to make disciples of the nations. Micah's prophecy serves as a wonderful encouragement to us. God will not only save the nations but also provide a way for them to become disciples!

> *...my house will be called*
> *a house of prayer for all nations*
> *(Isaiah 56:7b).*

What does it mean for God's house to become "a house of prayer for all nations?" First of all, it means that the nations will be welcome in His house. When we welcome people of different cultures into our worship times, we are helping to fulfill this prophecy. How would a visitor from another culture or language group feel if he or she visited your church? Would this one feel welcome to pray to God with you?

Secondly, it means that when believers meet together, they should learn how to pray for the nations that God so loves. They should provide specific prayer requests and other useful information for God's people to use in prayer. Ministers of the gospel should pray passionately for lost people of other languages and cultures around the world. New disciples should hear believers interceding for the unreached peoples of the world. Then God's house will truly be a house of prayer for all nations!

> *New disciples should hear believers interceding for the unreached peoples of the world.*

Prophecies Dealing with the Nations' Worship of God

The nations would be saved and discipled so that they too could worship the One Who is worthy — King Jesus! The prophets also saw the wonderful *worship* the peoples of the earth would offer to God. What a wonderful type of vision this is. They prophesied about it clearly:

> *"If you will return, O Israel, return to me," declares the Lord.*
> *'If you put your detestable idols out of my sight*
> *and no longer go astray,*
> *and if in a truthful, just and righteous way*
> *you swear, 'As surely as the Lord lives,'*
> *then the nations will be blessed by him*
> *and in him they will glory'*
> *(Jeremiah 4:1-2).*

Have you seen the nations "glorying" in the worship of the true God? God showed this to the prophets:

> *The Lord will be awesome to them*
> *when He destroys all the gods of the land.*
> *The nations on every shore will worship him,*
> *every one in its own land*
> *(Zephaniah 2:11).*

There is no need for the nations to make a difficult pilgrimage to a holy city. Every nation may worship in its own land. God will accept the worship and the offerings of people far away — even the people of Africa!

> *From beyond the rivers of Cush*
> *[that is, the upper Nile — Sudan and Ethiopia]*
> *my worshippers, my scattered people, will bring me offerings*
> *(Zephaniah 3:10).*

Prophecies Dealing with the Nations Working Together in the Missio Dei

The prophets also saw that these new worshippers from all nations would be joined to serve God together. They saw believers from every nation *working* together! Amazingly, the Scripture shows us a picture of something that is now occurring in God's harvest field. The prophet Zephaniah saw that nations would serve with one another in teams that would fulfill the *Missio Dei:*

> *Then will I purify the lips of the peoples,*
> *that all of them may call on the name of the Lord*
> *and serve him shoulder to shoulder*
> *(Zephaniah 3:9).*

Those who work "shoulder to shoulder" are working in trust, unity, and cooperation. It takes a miracle of God for people of different cultures to experience this level of mutual respect and partnership. The good news is that this miracle is happening in our day. We can be a part of it — if we humbly and gladly accept our co-laborers as they gather to serve the Lord from many different cultures and nations!

> *Many nations will be joined with the Lord in that day*
> *and will become my people*
> *(Zechariah 2:11a).*

Will you choose to form a common identity with the diverse teams that God is raising up in the last days? Jewish Barnabas was part of a

Gentile team in Antioch, and Jewish Paul worked with Luke the Greek. God may someday ask you to participate in a team like the one seen by Zephaniah!

The prophets were given a clear vision of the future of the nations. All the earth would one day respond to the Lord. His rule would expand, no longer limited to the Jews alone. How the prophets longed to see that day!

> *The Lord will be king over the whole earth.*
> *On that day there will be one Lord,*
> *and his name the only name*
> *(Zechariah 14:9).*

God's Servant the Messiah

The prophet Isaiah wrote one of the most moving and powerful books in the Bible. After his words of judgment came words of hope and restoration. In the last part of his book are four prophecies that are commonly called "The Servant Songs."

The Servant Songs spoke of a special Servant who would accomplish the great work of God's mission on earth. Part of the time the songs describe the work of God's people who should be His servants. However, many things in the Servant Songs could only be fulfilled by the long-awaited Son or offspring (seed, KJV) of the woman who would come to crush Satan (Genesis 3:15). The coming *Servant* or "seed" would be God's *Anointed One*, the Messiah!

> *Here is my servant, whom I uphold,*
> *my chosen one in whom I delight;*
> *I will put my Spirit on him*
> *and he will bring justice to the nations*
> *(Isaiah 42:1).*

Isaiah saw that the coming Messiah would be a humble servant whose work would affect more than just the people of Israel. The Servant would change the story of the nations.

> *"I, the Lord, have called you in righteousness;*
> *I will take hold of your hand.*
> *I will keep you and will make you*
> *to be a covenant for the people*
> ***and a light for the Gentiles,***
> *to open eyes that are blind,*
> *to free captives from prison*
> *and to release from the dungeon those who sit in darkness*
> *(Isaiah 42:6-7; emphasis mine).*

The Creator is now sending a special Servant to be a light for the Gentiles! In a later song, God says that this Servant must not be confined to a mission that is too small for Him:

> *It is too small a thing for You to be my servant*
> *to restore the tribes of Jacob*
> *and bring back those of Israel I have kept.*
> *I will also make you a light for the Gentiles,*
> *that you may bring my salvation to the ends of the earth*
> *(Isaiah 49:6).*

God the Father is speaking to the coming Messiah. He says that to save only one group of people would be a task too small for His Servant, the Messiah! Messiah was too great and His work too powerful to bless only one kind of people. Instead, God's anointed One will be sent to bring both Israel and the Gentiles to salvation. The same thing is true of believers in Christ, the church, who are the people of the Messiah today. They also exist to bring light not only to their own cultures but also to the ends of the earth.

Listen to another prophecy of Isaiah that reveals the words of Messiah himself:

> *The Sovereign Lord has given me an instructed tongue,*
> *to know the word that sustains the weary.*
> *He wakens me morning by morning,*
> *wakens my ear to listen like one being taught.*
> *The Sovereign Lord has opened my ears,*
> *and I have not been rebellious;*

> *I have not drawn back.*
> *I offered my back to those who beat me,*
> *my cheeks to those who pulled out my beard;*
> *I did not hide my face from mocking and spitting.*
> *Because the Sovereign Lord helps me,*
> *I will not be disgraced.*
> *Therefore have I set my face like a flint,*
> *and I know I will not be put to shame*
> *(Isaiah 50:4-7).*

What a magnificent vision of Jesus! The prophet Isaiah saw these vivid details about the life of Christ hundreds of years before Jesus was born. Isaiah also saw that obedient Servant would be abused by men. Still, the result of His life would not be disgrace. Instead, the Messiah declares that He will bring righteousness and enduring salvation:

> *Listen to me, my people;*
> *hear me, my nation:*
> *The law will go out from me;*
> *my justice will become **a light to the nations.***
> *My righteousness draws near speedily,*
> ***my salvation is on the way,***
> *and My arm will bring justice to the nations.*
> *The islands will look to me*
> *and wait in hope for my arm…*
> ***my salvation will last forever,***
> *my righteousness will never fail*
> *(Isaiah 51:4-5, 6b; emphasis mine).*

The light that was coming to the nations was not merely peace, provision, or comfort; it *was* the light of salvation. Messiah's work of salvation would last forever. God continued to reveal more of the *Missio Dei* to His servants the prophets.

Amos and David's Fallen Tent

The prophet Amos grew up as a shepherd and a farmer. He was not from a prophet's family, but God called him anyway (Amos 7:14-15). God sent him to prophesy concerning the future of the kingdom and the "charter for mankind" that had been promised to David:

> *"In that day I will restore David's fallen tent.*
> *I will repair its broken places, restore its ruins,*
> *and build it as it used to be,*
> *so that they may possess the remnant of Edom*
> *and all the nations that bear my name" declares the Lord,*
> *who will do these things*
> *(Amos 9:11-12).*

Amos' words help us understand what happened to the eternal kingdom promised to David. How could sons of David ever have been removed from the throne? How could Israel and Judah ever have been carried off into captivity? Hadn't God promised a kingdom that would last forever?

All nations bear God's name!

This prophecy makes it clear that although the "house" of David had become nothing more than a "fallen tent," God still planned to restore it. He would build it back! In addition, when God renewed David's "fallen tent," it would have an impact on "all the nations that bear My name" (Amos 9:12). David's house would rise again to bless the nations, just as God originally promised in His "torah/charter for mankind" (2 Samuel 7:19).

The phrase "all the nations that bear My name" is unusual and encouraging. It reminds us that people of all nations are made in God's image. People are allowed to write their name only on things that belong to them. To "bear God's name" means to belong to God.

None of these nations was serving God, yet still each one bore His name. There are still many nations and peoples today in the same situation. In spite of the failures of God's people, these nations must not be left out of God's promise plan.

God had not forgotten David's kingdom, and He had not forgotten His "charter" for the nations, either! Amos' prophecy connected the promise of David's restored kingdom to God's claim of ownership over Gentile nations.

This connection was very clear to Jewish readers. Hundreds of years later, James used this verse as evidence during a church council in the book of Acts. Some Jewish Christians did not want to accept the new Gentile converts into the church. There was much discussion. Perhaps there was no room for Gentiles in the church of Jesus Christ!

Then James quoted this very prophecy from Amos (see Acts 15:15-19). Jesus was restoring David's kingdom in an eternal, spiritual sense. The prophecy made clear that a restored "house" for David implied God's ownership of the Gentiles as well!

After James used this quotation, the problem was settled, and the Gentiles were accepted as brothers. David's promised kingdom was big enough to include the entire world. Praise God for Amos' clear understanding that all nations bear God's name!

Joel and the Holy Spirit Poured Out

The book of the prophet Joel is very helpful to pentecostal Christians. God spoke in advance to Joel about the outpouring of the Holy Spirit in the last days.

Joel's prophecies are very interesting. He first prophesied of a great swarm of locusts that would devour the harvest (Joel 1:1-2:17). After this disaster, God would take pity and pour out a new harvest on the land (Joel 2:18-27). These prophecies were the "harvest setting" that led directly into Joel's prophecy of the Spirit being poured out in the last days (Joel 2:28-29).

Why did Joel move from a locust plague to a prophecy of the Holy Spirit's outpouring? Just as God would restore the harvest of the earth after the plague of locusts, God would also pour out His Spirit to bring in the harvest of the nations after the plague of sin.

Joel's Prophecy Fulfilled

In the book of Acts, we discover that God chose to pour out His Spirit on the day of the Jewish harvest festival — the Day of Pentecost. Pentecost is always linked to Harvest!

Pentecost is always linked to Harvest!

Joel saw that an outpouring of the Spirit would take place that would bring all kinds of people into God's salvation plan:

> *And afterward, I will pour out my Spirit on* **all people.**
> *Your* **sons** *and* **daughters** *will prophesy,*
> *your* **old men** *will dream dreams,*
> *your* **young men** *will see visions.*
> *Even on my* **servants,** *both* **men** *and* **women,**
> *I will pour out my Spirit in those days…*
> *And* **everyone who calls** *on the name of the Lord will be saved…"*
> *(Joel 2:28-29, 32a; emphasis mine).*

Jeremiah prophesied that God would give a New Covenant to His people. Joel saw that the New Covenant would be given and that those who entered that covenant would also be able to experience personally the empowerment of the Spirit in a wonderful new way. All of God's people would become candidates to understand God's mission and to participate in it with prophetic power. Instead of writing its requirements on stone as He did in the days of Moses, God was going to write it on the people's hearts (see Jeremiah 31:33). Like Jeremiah, Joel saw that the New Covenant would involve people in a very personal connection with their God.

Joel also saw that this intimate connection with God's Spirit would be made available to every kind of person! Some of the groups of people mentioned, such as women and young people, were not often included in the move of the Holy Spirit in Old Testament times; however, Joel saw that this would change.

The new covenant would be effective where the old covenant had failed because God would make Himself known personally to all of His people.

> *For if there had been nothing wrong with that first covenant,*
> *no place would have been sought for another…*
> *"This is the covenant I will make with the house of Israel after that time…*
> *I will put my laws in their minds and write them on their hearts.*
> *I will be their God, and they will be my people.*
> *No longer will a man teach his neighbor,*
> *or a man his brother, saying 'Know the Lord,'*
> *because they all will know me,*

> *from the least of them to the greatest.*
> *For I will forgive their wickedness*
> *and will remember their sins no more"*
> *(Hebrews 8:7, 10-12).*

These words from the New Testament book of Hebrews are a quotation from Jeremiah 31:31-34. In both Jeremiah's and Joel's prophecies, God said that He would include all people. Praise God for His generous love. If all people had not been included, perhaps you or I would have been the one left out. Instead, we can all know the Lord!

When the Old Covenant was given, God showed his awesome power on Mount Sinai. The mountain shook with blazing fire and darkness and blasts from a heavenly trumpet. The sight filled the people with fear (Hebrews 12:18-21).

What power could God use to accomplish the new, more effective covenant?

Instead of trumpets in the heavens and flames on the mountain, God said He would reveal Himself inside of us. We would know Him in our own heart and mind (Jeremiah 31:33). We would feel Him moving in prophecy through our own mouths (Joel 2:28). The power would not be outside of us, but would be released into our own lives. God would give His people an outpouring of the Holy Spirit!

Pentecost: The Power for the New Covenant

The effective power behind the New Covenant would not be a sense of duty to the patriarchs or to the laws of religion. It would not be maintained by the performance of a few chosen prophets.

The power behind the New Covenant would be a dynamic, personal infilling of the Holy Spirit outpoured on all of God's people. What amazing words of prophecy these are. Hallelujah!

Anyone made in God's image can represent God. Joel saw a day when prophecy would not be limited to a small group of prophets. All of God's people would be able to hear His voice and declare His message to the world around them.

Neither age nor sex would any longer be a barrier. Men and women, young and old, would all be used alike by God in the great final days of salvation.

Everyone could be saved and everyone could be used by God. After all, everyone made in God's image is capable of knowing God's Spirit and being used by the Spirit.

Pentecost is not for a few key leaders or *stars* of the church. We must teach Pentecost, preach Pentecost, and practice Pentecost. A great part of ministry in the church is to mentor new believers in the proper use of the Pentecostal ministry gifts.

We do not believe in confusion; however, we do believe in access for all to the gifts of the Holy Spirit. Spiritual gifts must not be misused, but neither must they become extinct. The minister must not hold people back from being used by the Spirit. Instead, he or she should show the people how to walk in step with the Spirit.

Prayer #7

Almighty God,
Maker of the New Covenant,
I praise You for revealing Your power in a new way to mankind!
No longer must we gaze in terror
at a distant holy mountain, blazing with fire.
Instead, You have sent holy fire to blaze in our hearts!
We tremble with awe, yet rejoice with Your love.
You are writing Your word on our very hearts!
How amazing, how wonderful,
that all can know Your Holy Spirit.
Fill me, O Lord!
Fill all Your people.
Fill us with holy fire —
O Lord, fill us now!
Hallelujah!
Amen.

Figure 7.1

The gospel message is the good news of salvation in the New Covenant. When you cross cultural boundaries with the gospel, you can expect to see God pour out His Holy Spirit on the people of other cultures, too. They may respond to the Spirit in different ways than your people do, but the Holy Spirit will still be poured out on them. Pentecost is the central source of power for life in the New Covenant!

Partial Pentecost cannot fulfill the plan of God in the last days, for the work is great. As Joel shows us, Pentecost is always linked to Harvest. We need the Holy Spirit's fullness and power to do our part in the mission of God.

Jonah, the Reluctant Missionary

Jonah has a unique place in the development of the *Missio Dei*. God called this Old Testament prophet to go preach repentance to a Gentile nation (York, 61). God teaches us much through Jonah's response to the situation.

Instead of waiting for the nation of Assyria to come to the temple in Israel, God sent Jonah out to meet the Assyrians in their own country. Nineveh, their political capital, was a cruel city whose merciless armies had abused Israel in terrible ways. Jonah did not want to go there. His greatest fear was that someone would actually repent and be forgiven. Jonah wanted the Ninevites to suffer for their sins! For God to forgive the Ninevites would be a disaster, in Jonah's opinion.

Jonah should have remembered that God is King of the whole earth. As a result, he had to learn this lesson several times. He tried to argue with God's mercy, but the King would not change His mind. He also tried to run away from God on the sea, but found that God was King on the water just as much as on the land.

When God sent a storm, Jonah had to confess his sins against God to the Gentile sailors. These pagan sailors immediately showed their ability to pray to Jonah's God, in spite of their nationality. When Jonah was thrown overboard and swallowed alive by a great fish, he discovered that even in a fish's belly God could hear and answer prayer!

When Jonah finally went to Nineveh, he only shared half of God's message. Jonah's gospel was bad news, not good news. He walked up and down the streets of the city, preaching judgment without the possibility of mercy. Even then, God was able to produce a response in the hard-hearted people of Nineveh.

From the king down to the humblest subject, the people of whole city repented in sackcloth and prayed urgently to God. Jonah's God heard the Ninevites' prayers and withheld His judgment!

This was just what Jonah had feared. In the last chapter of the book, Jonah becomes terribly angry with God. He was more concerned with the withering of the vine that had given him shade than with the souls of the people of Nineveh. The last words of Jonah are the key to the entire book:

> *But the Lord said,*
> *"You have been concerned about this vine,*
> *though you did not tend it or make it grow.*
> *It sprang up overnight and died overnight.*
> *But Nineveh has more than a hundred and twenty thousand*
> *people who cannot tell their right hand from their left,*
> *and many cattle as well.*
> **Should I not be concerned about that great city**
> *(Jonah 4:10-11; emphasis mine).*

Who are the 120,000 people that God refers to? Some say that this number represents the population of Nineveh, but others feel that the phrase "people who cannot tell their right hand from their left" refers to the infants and young children of the families of the Ninevites. God's concern for children, for foreigners, and for sinners — even sinners from bad places! — is truly amazing.

The final words of Jonah are the main lesson of the book. God is speaking to Jonah, to Israel, and to all of us. He is telling us that we must care for the nations, even if they are our enemies.

He will not excuse us from reaching them. He will not excuse us for focusing on our own comfort instead of their eternal souls. God is concerned for every great and wicked city. We simply must be concerned for them as well.

Who wrote the book of Jonah? If it was written by the prophet himself, it may be safe to conclude that Jonah finally accepted the lesson God was teaching him. The book of Jonah is a powerful prophetic message to all those who would rather do something else instead of reaching out to ungodly Gentiles. We, like Jonah, must have a baptism of God's love and concern for our enemies and for places that we do not like.

The God who loves us also loves our enemies. God is concerned for the city!

Lessons from the Prophets

It is important to remember how surprising the prophets' words were to the people who heard them. They were messages of judgment, of holiness, of restoration for Jews, and inclusion for Gentiles. They were hard for the listeners to understand. Even the prophets themselves were amazed. They longed to understand fully what was coming next in God's great plan.

Many prophecies concerning the future have now been fulfilled. We should remember how privileged we are to live in the days when mysteries have been made clear!

All people who live with these privileges need to examine their lives often. We need to see if we are living in harmony with God's eternal plan.

> *Concerning this salvation,*
> *the prophets, who spoke of the grace that was to come to you,*
> *searched intently and with the greatest care,*
> *trying to find out the time and circumstances*
> *to which the Spirit of Christ in them was pointing*
> *when he predicted the sufferings of Christ and the glories that would follow.*
> *It was revealed to them that they were not serving themselves but you,*
> *when they spoke of the things that have now been told to you*
> *by those who have preached the gospel to you*
> *by the Holy Spirit sent from heaven.*
> *Even angels long to look into these things*
> *(1 Peter 1:10-12).*

We have the privilege to live on earth after the coming of the promised Messiah. Since the Bible is now complete, we may freely view the mysteries that prophets and angels longed to understand.

The *Missio Dei* is the greatest plan ever devised for mankind. Let us be careful to learn all we can and diligent to teach what we have learned to others!

Prayer #8

Lord Jesus,
Your sufferings are hard for us to understand
even on this side of the cross.
How difficult it must have been for the prophets!
Yet you still showed them visions of the glory of Your plan.
Salvation would come through a Servant.
Israel would be joined by the nations.
A New Covenant would be written —
not on stone, but on our hearts!
Lord, write Your plan on our hearts today!
May we never lose our amazement
about the mysteries that caused Your prophets
to "search intently, with greatest care."
In Your wonderful Name,
Amen!

Figure 7.2

Summary

The prophets had a two-fold duty. First, they were to call God's people to account for their sins and rebellion. However, they also saw with increasing clarity that the Messiah was coming to deal with the problem of sin. Second, they must declare the coming of the Messiah whom they longed to see because of the new covenant He would initiate. After their ministry, the stage was set for the appearance of Jesus Christ, the Savior of the World!

Review and Application

Now that you have completed your study of "the Messiah Foreseen in the Prophets," consider the implications of what you have learned. Seeing the realization of the *Missio Dei* in the message of the prophets should affect your preaching and teaching content as you seek to enlist others in God's mission. Will it have this effect in your ministry and service for God? I pray that it will.

1. Explain the point of the book of Jonah in your own words. If you were preaching a message from the book of Jonah, what specific call for response (altar call) would you give? Write it out below.

2. Why was it necessary for God to give a new source of power to His people when He gave them the new covenant?

3. How can the baptism in the Holy Spirit help us to remain close to God and effective in His mission? Discuss your answers with the class.

4. List the different groups of people in society who are mentioned by name in Joel's prophecy. Which group (or groups) do you belong to? How is God willing to use your group, according to the words of the prophet Joel?

5. How do you feel about being included in this prophecy? How would you feel if you were not included there? Discuss your answers with the class.

6. How would the future of the church have been different if the early Jerusalem church had not studied the book of Amos to find out God's position concerning the Gentile nations? How will the future of the church in your country be different if you do not make plans to win believers from foreign people groups? Discuss your answers in the class.

Be prepared to discuss these questions and any other questions or issues that come to mind when your instructor refers to them in class.

CHAPTER 8

The Messiah Arrives in the Gospels

*T*he New Testament opens with the wonderful news that the long-awaited Messiah has come. Jesus Christ is the King who came to live with His people. Jesus modeled the character of the Kingdom of God. When He lived among us, He not only gave us an example, but also died to pay the price for sin. The promise of the *Missio Dei* in the Old Testament will now be fulfilled in the life of Jesus Christ and those who become His disciples. The light of the world has come!

Matthew's Introduction

Four hundred years passed between the writing of the final Old Testament prophets and the coming of Jesus Christ. Some of the Jews returned from captivity in Babylon and rebuilt the city of Jerusalem. These Jews usually had freedom to live in their own land and to worship God. However, they fell under the control of the expanding Greek empire.

The Greeks used their money and influence to spread the Greek language and culture all around the known world. This process was called *hellenization*. Greek culture brought many new thoughts and lifestyles to Israel. Some Jews resented the changes that were being made to their traditional ways. This process is very similar to the "westernization" of cultures that is happening around the world today.

Later, the powerful Romans took over the Greek empire. Although they kept Greek culture and language, they ruled their colonies with a powerful military regime. No one could escape their control. Roman soldiers and their servants now ruled the land God had promised to Abraham!

The Jews longed to be free from foreign rule. They wondered when the Messiah would set up His eternal kingdom. During these years, the Jews read the words of the prophets and waited for their fulfillment. They were waiting for something important to happen.

The prophets had written with great expectation about the coming of the Messiah. They were aware of God's great promises to Abraham and David. They saw that the fulfillment of these great promises would come in the form of a person sent from God. The Jews anticipated the coming kingdom of the Messiah for centuries!

With this in mind, the opening words of the New Testament are very significant. Most readers skip over these names quickly without thinking about what they mean.

> *A record of the genealogy of Jesus Christ*
> *the son of David,*
> *the son of Abraham...*
> *(Matthew 1:1).*

Why, out of all the hundreds of characters in the Old Testament, are these two names included in the genealogy of Jesus? The names of Abraham and David are included for a reason. This short statement is an outline of the whole story of the *Missio Dei* in the Old Testament. Matthew is linking the story of Jesus Christ to the entire plan of the Mission of God which has already been told in the Old Testament.

Matthew begins by introducing "Jesus Christ." *Christ* means "the Anointed One." God has anointed Jesus as the Messiah!

What are this Messiah's credentials? Matthew explains who Jesus really is with the powerful claim that this Christ is first, the *Son of David* — which means He inherits David's promises of an eternal kingdom. Second, He is also the *Son of Abraham* — inheriting Abraham's promise to bless all nations.

Name in Matthew 1:1	*Jesus Christ*	*Son of David*	*Son of Abraham*
Significance of the name:	Anointed Messiah (Salvation)	Kingdom (Rule of God)	Blessing for Nations (*Missio Dei*)
Covenant implied in the name:	New Covenant (Jeremiah 31:31-34)	Davidic Covenant (2 Samuel 7:16)	Abrahamic Covenant (Genesis 12:1-3)

Figure 8.1

The Jews were waiting for a political Messiah to deliver them from the rule of the Roman Empire. They also longed for a Jewish Messiah to free them from the invasion of Greek culture. However, Jesus was not a political leader or cultural hero. He was coming to set up a different kind of kingdom.

Instead of governing people politically, Jesus was coming to transform their hearts. Instead of coming only to rule the Jews, Jesus was coming to bring salvation to people from every nation. This included Jews, Romans, Greeks, and all the peoples to the ends of the world.

This Jesus was the *seed of the woman,* the offspring promised in Genesis 3:15. His mission could not be confined culturally or politically. He was Eve's promised descendant who would be wounded by Satan, but who would finally crush that serpent's head. He was coming to save the peoples of the earth from their sin.

A King is Born

Jesus is the fulfillment of the entire story of the Old Testament! He is not a new idea from God; instead, He is the fulfillment of the promise God had been making from the very beginning.

The word *gospel* means "good news." The story of the coming of Jesus was good news for the nations from the very beginning:

> *After Jesus was born in Bethlehem in Judea,*
> *during the time of King Herod,*
> *Magi from the east came to Jerusalem and asked,*
> *"Where is the one who has been born king of the Jews?*
> *We saw his star in the east and have come to worship him"*
> *(Matthew 2:1-2).*

The Missio Dei was now being focused into the life of one Wonderful child. The nations were welcome at His birth!

The "*King* of the Jews" was seen and worshipped by "Magi from the East." Here, in typical gospel fashion, "kingdom" is connected to "nations." Foreign representatives had come to see the new King. This meant that David's kingdom (the infant King, Jesus) is saluted by Abraham's Blessing (the wise men from the East). The light of hope promised in the *Missio Dei* was now being focused into the brilliant life of one "Wonderful" child. The nations were welcome at His birth!

The child being born was of the greatest impact to the scattered peoples of the world. God announced this clearly through one of His faithful servants:

> *Now there was a man in Jerusalem called Simeon,*
> *who was righteous and devout.*
> *He was waiting for the consolation of Israel,*
> *and the Holy Spirit was upon him.*
> *It had been revealed to him by the Holy Spirit*
> *that he would not die before he had seen*
> *the Lord's Christ. (Luke 2:25-26)*

This man, Simeon, made a Spirit-led application of one of Isaiah's biblical prophecies. It is interesting to see that one of the first stories in the New

Testament is of a man being helped by the Holy Spirit to interpret correctly the Scripture. God is safeguarding His mission by sending the Spirit to give His people the correct understanding of the Bible!

> **Moved by the Spirit, he went into the temple courts.**
> *When the parents brought in the child Jesus*
> *to do for Him what the custom of the Law required,*
> *Simeon took him in his arms and praised God, saying:*
> *"Sovereign Lord, as you have promised,*
> *you now dismiss your servant in peace.*
> **For my eyes have seen your salvation,**
> **which you have prepared in the sight of all people,**
> **a light for revelation to the Gentiles**
> **and for glory to your people Israel"**
> *(Luke 2:27-32; emphasis mine).*

Now, at last, the "light for the Gentiles" was dawning on the world. The scattered families of nations would soon have a way of salvation. Soon the nations would begin to realize that *"this man really is the Savior of the world"* *(John 4:42b)*. No wonder the angels sang "Glory!" at His birth!

To understand the Gospels, you must read them with two themes in mind. These themes are brought to our mind when we remember two great characters from the Old Testament: Abraham and David. First, Jesus was coming to bring the long-awaited Kingdom of God (David's kingdom). Second, King Jesus was coming to bring about the long-awaited blessing of all nations (Abraham's blessing)! *Kingdom* and *Nations* are the twin themes of the good news, the gospel of Jesus Christ.

Kingdom and Nations in the Parables

Some of the most interesting verses of the Gospels are the parables of Jesus. Instead of teaching great systematic lectures, Jesus usually spoke to people using memorable stories that caused the hearers to ponder God's truth. A key purpose of the parables is to cause the hearers to think about the twin themes of *Kingdom* and *Nations* (York, 66).

Many parables begin with the words, "The kingdom of heaven is like…" (see Matthew 13:24, 13:31). They then go on to discuss some aspect of expansion or harvest. This harvest expansion will reach all nations.

> *The kingdom of heaven is like a mustard seed,*
> *which a man took and planted in his field.*
> *Though it is the smallest of all your seeds,*
> *yet when it grows, it is the largest of the garden plants and becomes a tree,*
> *so that the birds of the air come and perch in its branches*
> *(Matthew 13:31-32).*

Jesus used this story to help people realize that the Kingdom was here, and the Kingdom was going to grow! Another time, He told a parable that suggested that not everyone would be fit for the Kingdom.

> *Once again, the kingdom of heaven is like a net*
> *that was let down into the lake and caught all kinds of fish.*
> *When it was full, the fishermen pulled it up on the shore.*
> *Then they sat down and collected the good fish in baskets,*
> *but threw the bad away*
> *(Matthew 13:47-48).*

Jesus knew that the Kingdom would grow like a good harvest. He was trying to prepare workers who would be ready and motivated to gather that harvest in. The Kingdom is not about political control; instead, it is about harvest!

> *This is what the kingdom of God is like.*
> *A man scatters seed on the ground.*
> *Night and day, whether he sleeps or gets up, the seed sprouts and grows,*
> *though he does not know how.*
> *All by itself the soil produces grain —*
> *first the stalk, then the head, then the full kernel in the head.*
> *As soon as the grain is ripe, he puts the sickle to it,*
> *because the harvest has come.*
> *(Mark 4:26-29)*

Jesus did not raise up disciples so that they could take positions of power in the church (Mk 10:35-45). Instead, He raised up disciples so that they would do the work of harvest (York, 66-70). The message of salvation must be preached in all the world (Matthew 24:14). This is the business of the kingdom of God on earth!

Jesus raised up disciples so that they would do the work of harvest.

The Parable of the Sower

Two other parables of Jesus are so significant to a clear understanding of the *Missio Dei* that they will be covered here. These are the parables of the Sower and of the Eleventh Hour Laborers. These parables are master lessons of Jesus Christ. They are like golden keys that open the door of understanding about God's mission for us!

The parable of the Sower (the planter of seeds) is found in Matthew 13, Mark 4, and Luke 8. In this parable, Jesus used rich, visual words from daily events in the world that surrounded His listeners. These daily sights were familiar to everyone in the crowd. Here Jesus used the event of a farmer sowing seed as an enduring metaphor of what God's kingdom is like.

> *A farmer went out to sow his seed.*
> *As he was scattering the seed, **some fell along the path,***
> *and the birds came and ate it up.*
> ***Some fell on rocky places,** where it did not have much soil.*
> *It sprang up quickly, because the soil was shallow.*
> *But when the sun came up, the plants were scorched,*
> *and they withered because they had no root.*
> ***Other seed fell among thorns,** which grew up and choked the plants.*
> ***Still other seed fell on good soil,** where it produced a crop —*
> *a hundred, sixty, or thirty times what was sown.*
> *He who has ears, let him hear*
> *(Matthew 13:3-8; emphasis mine).*

Jesus is drawing a comparison between the activity of a farmer and the activity that takes place in the kingdom of God. Valuable seed will be "sown," or spread across the field, by untiring workers. The result will not always be the same because the soil is not the same. The difficulty is not with the seed, but the soil. Still, much soil will be productive and the harvest will be great.

Harvest is central to Jesus' teaching and to the kingdom of God.

You should remember two lessons from this parable. First, harvest is central to Jesus' teaching and to the kingdom of God. You cannot understand kingdom without understanding harvest. A church that is not involved in harvesting people does not have an applied understanding of the kingdom of God!

Second, the spreading of the Word of God (the "seed") will divide humanity into different groups. The Kingdom is not a kingdom that forces our obedience in this age. Instead, it is a kingdom that blesses all who willingly accept it. Not all people will respond to the seed so freely given to them.

In the kingdom of God, all people are offered the opportunity of blessing, but not all receive the blessing that could come to them. The prophets saw that this would be so:

> *Those who cling to worthless idols*
> *forfeit the grace that could be theirs…*
> *Salvation comes from the Lord.*
> *(Jonah 2:8, 9b)*

We would do well to remember these two lessons from the parable of the Sower, since Jesus said that this parable is key to understanding His other parables. Now read His words about the importance of the Parable of the Sower:

> *When He was alone, the Twelve and the others around Him*
> *asked Him about the parables…*
> *Then Jesus said to them, "Don't you understand this parable?*
> *How then will you understand any parable?"*
> *(Mark 4:10, 13).*

Jesus used parables to prepare kingdom workers for the task of spreading the seed of the Word of God. The people of the world would be separated by the different ways they responded to the good seed. The work of the kingdom of God consists of spreading the seed of God's Word onto all kinds of hearts in every kind of place!

The Parable of the Eleventh Hour Laborers

Those who work tirelessly in kingdom work may wonder about the success of their efforts. Many hearers do not respond well. The work is important, but it seems that it may never be finished. Kingdom workers may also wonder about their reward. This is the focus of the Parable of the Eleventh Hour Laborers.

> **Peter answered him, "We have left everything to follow you!**
> **What then will there be for us?"** *Jesus said to them,*
> *"I tell you the truth, at the renewal of all things,*
> *when the Son of Man sits on his glorious throne,*
> *you who have followed me will also sit on twelve thrones,*
> *judging the twelve tribes of Israel.*
> *And everyone who has left houses or brothers or sisters*
> *or father or mother or children or fields for my sake*
> *will receive a hundred times as much*
> *and will inherit eternal life"*
> *(Matthew 19:27-29; emphasis mine).*

Jesus answered Peter's question about rewards, but He did not want Peter to think that the work of the kingdom of God focused on this issue. So, he continued His reply to Peter's question by sharing the following parable:

> *But many who are first will be last, and many who are last will be first.*
> **The kingdom of heaven is like a landowner who went early in the morning**
> **to hire men to work in his vineyard.**
> *He agreed to pay them a denarius for the day and sent them out into his vineyard.*
> *About the third hour he went out*
> *and saw others standing in the marketplace doing nothing...*
> *He went out again about the sixth hour and the ninth hour and did the same thing.*
> *About the eleventh hour he went out and found still others standing around.*
> *He asked them, "Why have you been standing here all day long doing nothing?"*
> *"Because no one has hired us," they answered.*
> *He said to them, "You also go and work in my vineyard"*
> *(Matthew 19:30; 20:1-3, 5-7; emphasis mine).*

Peter was voicing the concern of the other apostles who wondered about what reward they might expect for following Jesus. Jesus assures them that there is a reward, but it is not what those on earth might assume. To explain, Jesus tells this striking parable.

The parable of the laborers tells a story that is tense with urgency. There is a harvest to be gathered, and it must be harvested today. Since delay will spoil the harvest, this is a time for action.

We see the landowner's urgency when we notice that he is personally involved in the searching for kingdom workers. The owner himself calls the workers. He is not satisfied with the progress and continues again and again to seek for new laborers until the very end of the day.

What he finds amazes him. In spite of the urgency of the harvest, not all are working! So, he continues to find potential workers that have not been given spiritual employment right up to the eleventh hour.

Yet at the end of the story the mood changes. Now, when the day is finished, the landowner is finally satisfied. In spite of earlier concerns, the harvest has indeed been gathered. Now it is time to pay the workers. However, Jesus' story is not over because the landowner rewards his workers in a way that is designed to reveal their motives for doing the work!

> *When evening came, the owner of the vineyard said to his foreman,*
> *"Call the workers and pay them their wages,*
> *beginning with the last ones hired and going on to the first."*
> *The workers who were hired about the eleventh hour came*
> *and each received a denarius.*
> *So when those came who were hired first, they expected to receive more.*
> *But each one of them also received a denarius.*
> *When they received it, they began to grumble…*
> *(Matthew 20:8-11).*

Imagine how interested Jesus' disciples must have been in this story! They could imagine those who worked hard all day long complaining about the equal wages of those who only began working in the eleventh hour. Why did the landowner pay both groups the same? As the disciples listened carefully, Jesus finished his story:

> But he answered one of them, "Friend, I am not being unfair to you.
> Didn't you agree to work for a denarius? Take your pay and go.
> I want to give the man who was hired last the same as I gave you.
> Don't I have the right to do what I want with my own money?
> Or are you envious because I am generous?"
> So the last will be first, and the first will be last
> (Matthew 20:13-16).

Now the disciples began to understand the point of Jesus' story. Jesus wanted them to ask themselves why they were working in the kingdom of God. Jesus was showing Peter that the most important thing is not the reward of the workers but rather the pleasure of the owner of the vineyard!

A kingdom worker realizes that the Owner has the right to do whatever He pleases. The kingdom worker also understands that the true joy of a worker is in pleasing the Owner and saving His precious harvest. The reward given by the Owner is both just and satisfying. The ones who worked the longest are rewarded well, and even the ones who worked the shortest time are fully rewarded by the generosity of the Owner.

There is another aspect of this parable that we also should understand. Notice that it was the eleventh hour laborers who completed the gathering of the harvest! We are living in the eleventh hour. We belong to a kingdom that has an urgent mission of harvest. The time of rest and reward has not yet arrived. This is the last moment for gathering the harvest of the earth. *This is the time for training a great workforce of eleventh-hour laborers.* Jesus' parable should burn into our hearts the urgency and significance of every moment in these last days. We do not need to worry about our wages because the Lord of the harvest is both fair and generous.

This is also the time for training a great workforce of eleventh-hour laborers. The task of preparing laborers for the harvest is essential. If new laborers do not arrive, the harvest will not be gathered. This concern was always present in Jesus' mind:

> *Then he said to his disciples,*
> *"The harvest is plentiful but the workers are few.*
> *Ask the Lord of the harvest, therefore,*
> *to send out workers into his harvest field"*
> *(Matthew 9:37-38).*

Those who the Lord of the harvest sends to work will need training, encouragement, and supervision. This is what Jesus did with the twelve disciples, and it is also what we must to do to help those whom God is calling today. The urgency of the harvest requires us to be concerned about developing workers in the eleventh hour!

Jesus' parable assures us that even in the eleventh hour, new workers can still be found. In fact, they will be the ones to complete the task! Let all God's kingdom workers rejoice that the harvest will be gathered successfully. Then we can share the generous reward, regardless of how long we have been working.

The harvest is worth saving, and the Owner is worthy of our best efforts. It is a privilege to serve in God's vineyard. We can trust the issue of rewards to Him.

Gentile References in the Gospels

We have already seen that Jesus' birth was well attended by Gentiles. The theme of Gentiles can be seen in many other places in the Gospels, as well.

Jesus said that a Gentile centurion had greater faith than any person found in Israel (Luke 7:9). Not only was this man a Gentile but also a member of the occupying Roman army! The Jews excluded such a person from worship at the temple, but Jesus made room for him in the kingdom of God. Jesus also was moved to action by the great faith of a Canaanite woman who was struggling with a case of demon possession in her family (Matthew 15:21-29).

Jesus and the Cleansing of the Temple

Another time, Jesus "cleansed the temple" by driving buyers and sellers from a market they had set up there. The area He cleansed was called the Court of the Gentiles. It was the only area where Gentiles could worship at the temple, but now it had been filled with those who were marketing goods for temple worship.

Jesus was furious that the Gentiles had been kept from praying to God by this misuse of their prayer area! The Gospel of Mark gives the full quotation of Isaiah 56:7 which Jesus used that day. It shows why Jesus was so angry. His concern was for the nations to have a place to pray when they came to the temple to seek for God.

> *On reaching Jerusalem, Jesus entered the temple area*
> *and began driving out those who were buying and selling there.*
> *He overturned the tables of the money changers*
> *and the benches of those selling doves,*
> *and would not allow anyone to carry merchandise through the temple courts.*
> *And as he taught them, he said,* **"Is it not written:**
> **'My house will be called a house of prayer for all nations'?**
> *But you have made it a 'den of robbers'"*
> *(Mark 11:15-17; emphasis mine).*

It was not just the making of a market that made Jesus angry. The place for the market angered Him. The Temple leaders had allowed the market to be held in the very place that Gentile seekers could come to pray. No other room was available for them. That is why Jesus cleared out their market. He was "cleansing" the court of the Gentiles so it could again be used for prayer by foreigners. Jesus was concerned about Gentiles who were spiritually hungry for God. In fact, He was about to die for sinners of all nations! If Jesus was willing to die for the Gentiles, He also certainly wanted them to have a place in God's temple to pray.

Jesus Is the Light of the World

The Gospel of John is quite different from Matthew, Mark, and Luke. John is thought to have been the youngest apostle, and he wrote his gospel late in his life. He had most of his life to think about Who Jesus was. By the time he wrote, he had spent a lifetime serving the Kingdom of God. He was also able to think carefully about the words he used as he wrote the story of Jesus Christ.

John frequently used a word that reminds us of the mission of God. Thirty-six times John used the Greek word *kosmos,* which in English is translated "world" or "inhabited world" (York, 72). Jesus was King of not just Israel, but of the entire inhabited world.

> *The true light that gives light to every man was coming into the world.*
> *He was in the world, and though the world was made through him,*
> *the world did not recognize Him...*
> *Yet to all who received him, to those who believed in his name,*
> *he gave the right to become children of God*
> *(John 1:9-10, 12).*

Jesus was entering the world, and His entrance would bring salvation everywhere. John also used the word *kosmos* in one of the most famous passages of his Gospel:

> *For God so loved the world that he gave his one and only Son,*
> *that whoever believes in him shall not perish but have eternal life.*
> *For God did not send his Son into the world to condemn the world,*
> *but to save the world through him.*
> *Whoever believes in him is not condemned,*
> *but whoever does not believe stands condemned already*
> *because he has not believed in the name of God's one and only Son*
> *(John 3:16-18).*

John makes a progressive teaching in this passage. First, God loves the world. Second, God sent his Son into the world. Third, if the people of the world do not believe in God's Son Jesus, they are "condemned already" because they have no relationship with God's Son. Their danger is not just in the future; it is also in the present (John 3:18). Fourth, in spite of the danger of condemnation, there is hope in Jesus: the world can be saved through Him! John's four points are a wonderful outline of the gospel message. This is the message that we are called to preach to people everywhere.

John saw the world in much worse danger than we would like to believe. The world is condemned already; however, he also saw a gospel that was much more wonderful than we have yet realized. In spite of its sin and mankind's current state of condemnation, "God so loved the world!"

Jesus and the Samaritan Woman

Jesus made one of the clearest statements of who He is in John chapter 4. The recipient of this amazing revelation was not a Jew, a godly man, or even a man at all. It was the Samaritan woman.

> *The Samaritan woman said to him,*
> *"You are a Jew and I am a Samaritan woman.*
> *How can you ask me for a drink?"*
> *(For Jews do not associate with Samaritans.)*
> *Jesus answered her, "If you knew the gift of God*
> *and who it is who asks you for a drink, you would have asked him*
> *and he would have given you living water…"*
> *The woman said, "I know that Messiah" (called Christ) "is coming.*
> *When he comes, he will explain everything to us." Then Jesus declared,*
> *"I who speak to you am he" (John 4:9-10, 25-26).*

Jesus' interaction with the Samaritan woman is a model of His burden for the lost people of the world. Although Jews detested the Samaritans, He made His way to her town. Even though she was a woman, He spoke to her in a respectful and affirming way. Although she was a noted sinner, He offered her the water of life. When she expressed her hope in the coming of the Messiah, Jesus told her directly the most amazing thing of all:"I who speak to you am He" (v. 26).

Rarely did Jesus ever speak so clearly about His identity as He did to this foreign woman! No Rabbi or Pharisee ever heard Him say such words.

Her town had already given up on her as a hopeless case, but Jesus saw her as a lost soul made in God's image. She was "condemned already," but she was still a candidate to receive eternal life. So He told her Who He was!

The rest of the story shows that she did indeed find life by believing in God's Son, and she led many others to eternal life, as well. The clarity of their understanding of Jesus Christ is amazing. The half-Jewish Samaritans claimed Jesus as their own Savior, because He was the Savior "of the world"!

> *Many of the Samaritans from that town believed in him*
> *because of the woman's testimony...they said to the woman,*
> *"We no longer believe just because of what you said;*
> *now we have heard for ourselves, and we know*
> *that* **this man really is the Savior of the world"**
> *(John 4:39, 4; emphasis mine).*

Jesus and "The Other Sheep"

John also gives us a valuable account of Jesus' own sense of His mission in John 10. Here, Jesus calls Himself the Good Shepherd. He not only cares for the sheep in His flock but also longs to find those who have wandered from His care.

> *I am the good shepherd;*
> *I know my sheep and my sheep know me...*
> *and I lay down my life for the sheep.*
> *I have other sheep that are not of this sheep pen.*
> *I must bring them also*
> *(John 10:14, 15b-16a).*

In saying that He would lay down His life for His sheep, Jesus reminds us of Isaiah's understanding of the Suffering Servant. The eternal life that Jesus was offering to the world would come at a terrible cost. Jesus knew from the beginning that He was sent to die on a cross for the sins of the world.

What kept Jesus on course to pay the terrible price for sin? Why did He go all the way to the cross? This passage helps us understand what was in Jesus' heart. The Mission of God always drove Jesus forward. He refused to forget the "other sheep" who were not from "this sheep pen" (this culture and this place). The only way they could be saved was if He finished the work of redemption on the cross, and then sent out messengers to tell the whole world of His offer of salvation. Jesus kept His eyes on the "other sheep" and insisted "I must bring them also."

Other places in the Bible show us this motivation of Jesus as well. Hebrews says "Let us fix our eyes on Jesus...who for the joy set before him endured the cross" (Hebrews 12:2). Revelation shows us the heavenly worshippers saying, "You are worthy...with your blood you purchased men for God from every tribe and language…" (Revelation 5:9). During His life, Jesus meditated on Old Testament Scriptures such as the second Psalm:

> *"Ask of me, and I will make the nations your inheritance,*
> *the ends of the earth your possession…*
> *Kiss the Son, lest he be angry…*
> *Blessed are all who take refuge in him"*
> *(Psalm 2:8, 12).*

The joy that caused Jesus to endure was the promised reward of seeing the "other sheep" gathered into the Father's eternal home! All those who love Jesus must also learn to love and serve the "other sheep" who are so important to Him.

Jesus and the Greek Visitors

Late in Jesus' ministry, some Greeks came to see Him. This was an unusual event because Jesus had been sent to live among the Jews, and the Great Commission had not yet been given to the twelve disciples. It appears that the Greeks came too early. They came first to Philip, who had a Greek name. Then Philip and Andrew took their request to Jesus, not knowing how He would answer. As usual, Jesus had something interesting to say; however, His response is hard to understand at first.

> ***Now there were some Greeks*** *among those*
> *who went up to worship at the Feast.*
> *They came to Philip…with a request.*
> **"Sir," they said, "we would like to see Jesus."** *Philip went to tell Andrew;*
> *Andrew and Philip in turn told Jesus.*
> *Jesus replied, "The hour has come for the Son of Man to be glorified.*
> *I tell you the truth, unless a kernel of wheat falls to the ground and dies,*
> *it remains only a single seed.*
> *But if it dies, it produces many seeds…*
> **But I, when I am lifted up from the earth, will draw all men to myself."**
> *He said this to show the kind of death he was going to die*
> *(John 12:20-24, 32-33; emphasis mine).*

When Andrew and Philip told Jesus that Greeks were trying to see Him, Jesus spoke in reply about His own death. His reply means that there was something additional that had to happen before the spiritually hungry Greeks could be satisfied. Because the Greeks were coming to Him "ahead of schedule," Jesus knew that the time had come for Him to complete the work of world redemption. Notice how focused Jesus was on His mission to save the world!

The Gentiles did not need a new ethical teaching or another religious interview; they needed a Savior. If Gentiles were already coming to see Jesus, then Jesus realized that it was time for Him to purchase their salvation by His blood on the cross. How humbling that Jesus would lay down His own life to "produce many seeds" and "draw all men" to Himself!

The Cross and the Empty Tomb

> *The death and resurrection of Jesus Christ form the central point of the Mission of God.*

The death and resurrection of Jesus Christ form the central point of the mission of God, and also of all human history. Everything before Christ's death and resurrection looked forward to the day when God would perform the work of redemption for lost humanity. Everything after these events points back to the one way of salvation through Jesus Christ.

Our Lord died to take away our sins and rose again so that we also might live. He was not obligated to do anything to save us since we were the ones who had broken covenant. However, He freely chose to do everything that we would ever need.

It was a man from Africa who carried Jesus' cross to the place of crucifixion (Luke 23:26). After Christ had been mocked and severely beaten, the Roman soldiers crucified Him along with two criminals. They drove iron spikes through the small bones of His wrists and ankles until He was fastened to the tree.

Although the pain was great, death on the cross could take many days. Even then, Jesus was thinking of forgiveness instead of justice. "Jesus said, 'Father, forgive them, for they do not know what they are doing." (Luke 23:34a). At the place of execution, many people stood staring at Jesus' agony. He hung naked on the cross as the rulers jeered at Him.

> *The people stood watching, and the rulers even sneered at him.*
> *They said, "He saved others, let Him save himself*
> *if he is the Christ of God, the Chosen One."*
> *…There was a written notice above him, which read:*
> *THIS IS THE KING OF THE JEWS.*
> *One of the criminals who hung there hurled insults at him:*
> *"Aren't you the Christ?*
> *Save yourself and us!" (Luke 23:35, 38-39).*

The notice above His head was meant to mock Him; however, Jesus was in fact the King, just as it said. The first criminal was insulting Christ by asking him to save. How amazing to note that Jesus was in fact doing the work of salvation at the very moment that the criminal was mocking Him! Jesus died even for the very ones who tried to make His death more miserable.

The second crucified criminal had faith to believe in Jesus Christ. He rebuked the first criminal and spoke respectful words to Jesus. The Lord's reply can give hope to us all:

> *But the other criminal rebuked him.*
> *"Don't you fear God…since you are under the same sentence?*
> *…this man has done nothing wrong…*
> *Jesus, remember me when you come into your kingdom."*
> *Jesus answered him, "I tell you the truth,*
> *today you will be with me in paradise"*
> *(Luke 23:40a, 41b-43).*

Even while dying, Jesus was attracting people to the kingdom of God. He kept His focus on the lost of every nation and the salvation He wanted to offer to them. He continued doing the work of the kingdom until the very end.

Jesus stepped from the agony of the cross to the glory of the throne. The Lamb slain for the sin of the world became the King of kings and Lord of lords (Revelation 19:16)! The greatest deed of history was accomplished!

> *And when Jesus had cried out again in a loud voice, he gave up His spirit.*
> *At that moment the curtain of the temple was torn in two from top to bottom.*
> *The earth shook and the rocks split…*
> *When the centurion and those with him who were guarding Jesus*
> *saw the earthquake and all that had happened,*
> *they were terrified, and exclaimed,*
> *"Surely he was the Son of God!"*
> *(Matthew 27:50-51, 54).*

Hands from above tore the curtain of the temple from top to bottom, revealing the Holy Place that had always been hidden before. In the Old Testament, no ordinary worshipper could enter God's holy presence, but Jesus' death changed that:

> *Therefore, brothers, since we have confidence*
> *to enter the Most Holy Place by the blood of Jesus,*
> *by a new and living way opened for us through the curtain,*
> *that is, his body,*
> *and since we have a great priest over the house of God,*
> *let us draw near to God with a sincere heart in full assurance of faith…*
> *(Hebrews 10:19-22a).*

Perhaps we Christians speak too lightly of the cross. It is a mysterious and terrible thing to ponder the death of the Son of God. Many questions should come to our minds as we think about what Jesus did for the world there.

- Who are we to expect that we should be saved?
- Why should anyone die in our place?
- How could God send His only Son to die?
- Why should Jesus lay down His life for His enemies?
- How could the Giver of life ever die?
- How did the Son survive the moment when the Father turned His face away?
- What kind of power is this that raised Christ from the dead?
- How can one as great as Jesus now live in our hearts by faith?

The mystery of the cross may never be fully understood by human intellect. However, we can still be saved and called to serve by the wonder of the cross of Christ. We must remember that Christ's death and resurrection are the holy mystery at the very heart of the *Missio Dei*. God is on a mission, and Christ carried out His role in that plan to the very end. We are called to carry out our role in His mission, as well (York, 176).

Jesus was buried by a man who "was waiting for the kingdom of God" (Luke 23:51), Joseph of Arimathea. Jesus' body was wrapped and laid in Joseph's own unused tomb on Friday evening; however, His body did not lay there for long!

> *...at dawn on the first day of the week,*
> *Mary Magdalene and the other Mary went to look at the tomb.*
> *There was a violent earthquake, for an angel of the Lord came down from*
> *heaven and, going to the tomb, rolled back the stone and sat on it...*
> *The angel said to the women, "Do not be afraid, for*
> *I know you are looking for Jesus, who was crucified.*
> *He is not here; he has risen, just as he said.*
> *Come and see the place where He lay...*
> *Now I have told you" (Matthew 28:1-2, 5-6, 7b).*

Praise the Lord! Jesus suffered the worst fate that hell could prepare, and it was not enough to hold Him. The tomb is empty, and no one has ever found the body of our Lord. Jesus lives forever by the power of God!

"Now there is hope for any sinner in any nation"

Because He lives, we also can live. Now there is hope for any sinner in any nation. Now the way to God, symbolized by the curtain, has been opened for whoever desires to come. Now the Greeks are free to come searching for peace with God. The cross and the empty tomb are the centerpiece of the great mission of God. The work of salvation is finished for all who will believe!

Prayer #9

> *O Jesus Christ,*
> *What can I say?*
> *You have done more to save me than I ever dreamed.*
> *I gave You my guilt and You gave me Your glory.*
> *I gave You my debt and You gave me great deliverance.*
> *I gave You my shame and You gave me sweet redemption.*
> *You died for me —*
> *Help me to live for You!*
> *In Your own precious Name I pray,*
> *Amen.*

Figure 8.2

The Great Commission

A commission is a strategic task that a leader assigns his representatives to complete. However, the commission must be accompanied by the power and the delegated authority to do the task. Jesus gave all believers a commission from God Himself.

> *A commission is a strategic task that a leader assigns his representatives to complete.*

After Jesus' resurrection, He appeared to the eleven disciples — appeared before them in a locked room — alive and in the flesh. He certainly had their attention!

At first the disciples were afraid, but their fear turned to amazement and joy. Then Jesus spoke words to them that would shape their lives, as well as our own. Jesus gave His disciples a commission.

It is the greatest single task that God has ever delegated to mankind. He is naming us as His representatives in the *Missio Dei*. While Adam was given the task of describing the first creation, we are given the task of telling people about the New Creation!

We have been sent to spread the best news the world has ever heard. That is why these words are often called the "Great Commission."

> *All authority in heaven and on earth has been given to me.*
> **Therefore go and make disciples of all nations,**
> *baptizing them in the name of the Father and of the Son and of the Holy Spirit,*
> *and teaching them to obey everything I have commanded you.*
> *And surely I am with you always, to the very end of the age*
> *(Matthew 28:18-20; emphasis mine).*

Jesus first of all told the disciples that He had been given all authority in heaven and on earth. What a dramatic statement! Since He had just triumphed over death, it was clearly true.

It is true that never has any president or emperor assigned a more difficult task to be done. It is also true that never has any leader provided greater resources to his representatives to help them accomplish the task! Jesus is literally telling us that if we obey Him, all authority on heaven and earth will be released to support our efforts.

Authority is a word that implies kingdom. The risen Christ is King over heaven and earth. There is literally nothing that can stand in His way. We should not hesitate to gladly serve such a King. He has the power to make our obedient service to succeed!

The Commission to Make Disciples

After making His authority and Kingship clear, Jesus gave a central command. The Great Commission is a long sentence with several verbs that require action. In the English text, it appears that the main verb in the Great Commission is *Go*. However, this is not true. In the Greek sentence, the main verb is *Make Disciples*. The other verbs are in the sentence to tell us *how* to make the new disciples that Christ requires.

Making disciples is much more than simply making converts, just as raising children is much different than simply giving birth to children. Conversion may sometimes take place in a brief moment, but discipleship requires time. Discipleship also requires the help of a "disciple-maker" who will both teach and show the disciple what kind of person he or she is to become.

You cannot leave out the disciple-maker and still produce disciples. In fact, Jesus said that a disciple is someone who fully resembles his or her master. "A student is not above his teacher, but everyone who is fully trained will be like his teacher" (Luke 6:40). A true disciple thinks like, talks like, walks like, and acts like his or her master. A disciple of Jesus must think, talk, walk, and act like Christ!

How can a new believer learn to closely resemble Jesus when Jesus has already returned to His throne in heaven? There must be examples for that new believer to see and follow. Disciples need to belong to a caring and godly community. Disciples need someone called to the ministry of disciple-making to come alongside their life and help them over the difficult places.

Making disciples is what we are commissioned to do.

Although making converts is relatively easy in some cultures, making disciples always takes much time, personal contact, real love, and long-term dedication. However, this is what we are commissioned to do.

We have been commissioned to walk closely with sincere disciples until they resemble the Master. The people we are called to disciple are not only people from our own culture but also those from "every nation!"

Studying the Meaning of the Great Commission

One way to study a Scripture passage is to look for a word or idea that is repeated in the text. Repetition in Scripture often shows us the structure of the verse being studied. In the Great Commission in Matthew 28, look for the words "all," "every," and "always." Now notice how often Jesus used the word or idea *all:*

- All authority   (belongs to God)
- All nations   (must be discipled)
- All included   (in the church by baptism)
- All teaching   (must be passed on)
- All time   (God will be with us)

Jesus Christ is the Lord of "All!" He has "all authority" and He is the "Lord of all the earth." He died to include "all nations" in His heavenly family. He wants us to pass on all of His teachings to the nations. As we obey Him, He will be with us for all time! The Great Commission is a powerful statement of the *Missio Dei*. In all nations, the Good News must be preached and disciples must be made.

The final promise of God's enduring presence is the greatest joy of the Christian life. All nations must be discipled, and God will be with us until the work is done!

Sometimes we miss the full meaning of a well-known Scripture because we are too familiar with its words. In such cases, it may help to restate the familiar verses, or to translate them into another language you know well. Christ's Great Commission could be restated in the following way:

JESUS' COMMISSION TO HIS SERVANTS
I have been given the rightful power to rule over all the glories of heaven and all the nations of the earth. As King, I now give you this solemn Charge: ***Make Disciples of All Nations!***
I have left you my example of how to do this work. In order to make disciples of all nations: ***You must Go*** to the places where the nations are, ***You must Baptize*** them as full members of my church, and ***You must Teach*** them to know and follow all the lessons I first taught you.
This Commission is to become your life Work, your constant Prayer, your new Identity! And as you labor, never forget: ***I Will Always Be With You,*** until this age ends and heaven's joys begin!

Figure 8.3

Long before, Joshua faced a difficult commission given to him by Moses. Joshua took courage in the fact that God would always be with him as he worked to take the land. Like Joshua, we too can now be sure of God's manifest presence if we advance in the direction of the will of God. If we set out to make disciples of the nations, God will always be with us!

Summary

The Gospels are the good news of salvation through Jesus Christ. The themes of kingdom and nations are found throughout the Gospels. Jesus used parables as ways of teaching the essential theme of harvest expansion in the kingdom of God. Jesus ministered to the Gentiles in many ways in the Gospels and kept His focus clear all the way to the cross.

The death and resurrection of Jesus Christ are the central point of human history, and the center of the *Missio Dei*. After rising from the dead, Jesus appeared to His disciples and commissioned them to make disciples of all nations on earth. We also have received this commission from Christ. As we continue to make disciples of all nations, He has assured us of His authority and His ongoing presence in our lives.

Review and Application

Now that you have completed your study of the Messiah's arrival in the Gospels, ask yourself this question: "How may I incorporate my Master's goal and passion for the lost into my study, prayer life and plans for ministry and service?"

1. Which prophecy of Isaiah did Simeon, the godly elder, quote on Jesus' dedication day? Give the reference.

2. Discuss ways in which Jesus fulfilled both the promise to Abraham and the promise to David.

3. Explain the key ideas in the Parable of the Sower that can help us to understand Jesus' other parables, as well.

4. Are you an eleventh-hour laborer in the kingdom of God? Explain your answer.

5. As a group, list seven ways that you could become involved in a new believer's life in order to obey Christ's command to "make disciples of all nations." Do not include "attending church" in your list — think of other ways to make a disciple beyond simple church attendance.

6. How do you feel about your calling knowing that in fact, Christ has ALL authority in heaven and on earth? Explain.

Be prepared to discuss these questions and any other questions or issues that come to mind when your instructor refers to them in class.

Unit 4
The Culmination of the Missio Dei

CHAPTER 9

God's Mission Narrated in the Book of Acts

A fter Jesus' resurrection, the disciples felt the urgency of their commission. Jesus had died and risen again. God had established the means by which He could forgive people of their sins. However, the world did not immediately respond to Christ's work on the cross. After all, most of the world did not yet know the story!

The disciples had been left the task of informing the world of the salvation to be found in Christ. In addition, they were to make new disciples of all those who believed. The power to do this work was not found in the workers themselves, but in the dynamic, ongoing presence of the Holy Spirit.

As the believers reached out into the world, they would be fulfilling their role in the Mission of God. As the people of the world heard and accepted the message, they would begin to be blessed by Jesus, the Seed of Abraham. God's promise to Abraham is beginning to be fulfilled! The thrilling story is told in the book of Acts and the missionary letters that follow it.

The Acts of the Holy Spirit

The book of Acts describes the activities of the apostles and the churches immediately after the Great Commission was given. Acts is the story of how the Holy Spirit worked powerfully through the church to bless the nations.

Some English Bibles choose to call this book "The Acts of the Apostles." Perhaps a better name is "The Acts of the Holy Spirit through the Believers." Acts is a book dedicated to showing how the Holy Spirit moves through God's commissioned representatives as they obey the calling of God.

Acts tells many true stories about miracles, and these accounts are normative (York, 181-182). This means that they describe the way things should continue to happen in the future.

If the ministry in Acts was not meant to be repeated, it could be classified as a story of historical interest for Christian scholars. However, since the process described is normative, the principles found in Acts can be used to train new generations of eleventh-hour laborers.

The book of Acts is the study manual for the last day harvest expansion of the kingdom of God. Ministers today can understand its principles and apply its lessons about the empowerment of the Holy Spirit. All those who walk in step with the wonderful Holy Spirit will be blessed!

The Power to Perform God's Mission

In his book *Empowered for Global Mission,* missionary and author Denny Miller explains the central lesson of the book of Acts. There is a cycle (or process of activity) that repeats seven times in the book. This cycle involves both the Holy Spirit and the believers.

God begins the cycle by giving a divine gift of Holy Spirit empowerment to His disciples at a definite moment. Then disciples completed the cycle by going out in spiritually effective witness. *Holy Spirit Empowerment leading directly to Witness* is the key process of the book. This is the normative ministry dynamic that the book of Acts teaches (Miller, 20).

Divine Power at Pentecost

Jesus trained the disciples for three years. They had witnessed His death on the cross and His powerful resurrection. They had also been given Jesus' specific command to make disciples of all nations; however, all this was not enough. Jesus told the disciples to wait for one additional and necessary gift from heaven:

> *On one occasion, while he was eating with them,*
> *he gave them this command:*
> *"Do not leave Jerusalem, but wait for the gift my Father promised,*
> *which you have heard me speak about.*
> *For John baptized with water,*
> *but in a few days you will be baptized with the Holy Spirit"*
> *(Acts 1:4-5).*

Later He made sure that the disciples understood the purpose of this promise. The baptism in the Holy Spirit would give them the power to witness at home and to all the nations (York, 182-183)!

But you will receive power when the Holy Spirit comes on you;

> *and you will be my witnesses in Jerusalem,*
> *and in all Judea and Samaria,*
> *and to the ends of the earth*
> *(Acts 1:8).*

Jesus was telling His disciples that the *Missio Dei* to the "ends of the earth" would be powered not by human effort, but by the gift of the Holy Spirit.

The disciples were saved because of the power of the cross. Their eternal life was demonstrated by Christ's resurrection. However, they did not yet demonstrate miraculous authority in ministry, for they were still hidden away in an upper room. Their great spiritual power came to them a few weeks later, on the day of the Feast of Pentecost.

> *When the day of Pentecost came, they were all together in one place.*
> *Suddenly a sound like the blowing of a violent wind came from heaven*
> *and filled the whole house where they were sitting.*
> *They saw what seemed to be tongues of fire*
> *that separated and came to rest on each of them.*
> *All of them were filled with the Holy Spirit*
> *and began to speak in tongues as the Spirit enabled them*
> *(Acts 2:1-4).*

This was a powerful experience that fundamentally changed the lives of everyone present. The apostles had entered the prayer meeting with salvation, with eternal hope, and with a great commission. They and all of the believers present left the meeting with divine power to minister to people — even people from other languages and cultures.

Gentile Languages at Pentecost

The list of Gentile tongues spoken aloud on the Day of Pentecost is significant. The Spirit was being given to those who believed from every nation!

> *Now there were staying in Jerusalem*
> *God-fearing Jews from every nation under heaven.*
> *When they heard this sound, a crowd came together in bewilderment,*
> *because each one heard them speaking in his own language...*
> *"Parthians, Medes and Elamites;*
> *residents of Mesopotamia, Judea and Cappadocia,*
> *Pontus and Asia, Phrygia and Pamphylia,*
> *Egypt and the parts of Libya near Cyrene;*
> *visitors from Rome...Jews and converts...Cretans and Arabs —*
> *we hear them declaring the wonders of God in our own tongues!"*
> *(Acts 2:5-6, 9-11).*

God had poured an entirely new experience of His indwelling power into the disciples. He had also arranged for a crowd of people newly arrived from the ends of the earth to gather. These people thought they had traveled to Jerusalem for the Jewish feast of harvest or *Pentecost*. God had actually gathered the nations to His Pentecostal "feast of fire"!

The Power for Pentecostal Preaching

The disciples had not been able to stand with Christ at His arrest and crucifixion because of their weakness and fear. Like Peter, they often were not sure what to say. Now, God's anointing blazed like a flame from heaven in their hearts. With the empowerment of the baptism in the Holy Spirit, everything was different:

> *Then Peter stood up with the Eleven, raised his voice*
> *and addressed the crowd:*
> *"Fellow Jews and all of you who live in Jerusalem,*
> *let me explain this to you...this is what was spoken by the prophet Joel:*
> *'In the last days, God says, I will pour out my Spirit on all people.*
> *Your sons and daughters will prophesy,*
> *your young men will see visions,*
> *your old men will dream dreams.*
> *Even on my servants, both men and women, I will pour out my Spirit*
> *in those days, and they will prophesy...*
> *And everyone who calls on the name of the Lord will be saved"'*
> *(Acts 2:14, 16-18, 21).*

Peter stood with the other apostles and boldly addressed the crowd. His words were prophetically anointed, just as the prophet Joel predicted. The message was powerful, persuasive, and filled with the solid truth of the Scripture because the Holy Spirit was helping him. The Scriptures and their meanings were flowing clearly from his mouth, and the people were listening.

Peter explained that the sound of Gentile tongues which confused the crowd was in fact the fulfillment of a prophecy. It was the evidence of the end-time outpouring of the Holy Spirit prophesied by Joel!

Remember, Joel's unique prophecy told of a locust plague that destroyed the harvest. Joel saw that God would take pity and restore the harvest to his people. Next, Joel immediately prophesied an outpouring of the Holy Spirit that would result in a "harvest" of salvation (Joel 2:28-32). For Joel, the outpouring of the Holy Spirit is connected to the Harvest. This is why God fulfilled Joel's prophetic words on the feast of harvest — the Day of Pentecost.

Peter recognized that God had begun the outpouring that would help bring in the harvest! The time had come for everyone to call on the name of the Lord for salvation (Joel 2:32). So, Peter boldly began to preach with prophetic power. His divinely inspired message is still a wonderful model for the preaching of the gospel today.

The Content of the Apostles' Preaching

The content of his sermon was simple: Jesus Christ was sent from God, was crucified, was resurrected, and is now glorified! It was a message that powerfully called for everyone who heard it to repent.

> *Jesus of Nazareth was a man accredited by God to you by miracles…*
> *This man was handed over to you…and you, with the help of wicked men,*
> *put him to death by nailing him to the cross.*
> *But God raised him from the dead…*
> *God has made this Jesus, whom you crucified, both Lord and Christ…*
> *Repent and be baptized, every one of you, in the name of Jesus Christ*
> *for the forgiveness of your sins.*
> *And you will receive the gift of the Holy Spirit.'*
> *(Acts 2:22b, 23b-24a, 36b, 38b)*

The points of this first sermon are the core of gospel preaching throughout the book of Acts. Peter preached the coming, death, resurrection, glorification, and the present Lordship of Jesus Christ.

Bible scholars call these essential points of the gospel the *kerygma*. We should still preach each of these points clearly today. The content of our message matters. If you are going to preach, be sure you are preaching the gospel! Do not add extra requirements to the gospel, and do not leave any part of it out.

The Anointing to Call for a Response

The Holy Spirit clearly anointed the content and the wording of Peter's sermon. The Spirit also enabled Peter to give a clear and powerful call for response. The ability to give such a clear, effective call for response is evidence of the Spirit's enablement.

An effective altar call is not just the work of the preacher. As the preacher gives the altar call, he or she must cooperate with what the Holy Spirit is doing in the lives of the listeners.

The hearers are experiencing a supernatural work of God in their own hearts. The preacher respects God and respects the listeners, too. So the preacher must listen to the voice of the Holy Spirit in order to know what to do.

A Spirit-led altar call is not a guessing game. It should not be unclear or weak, but powerful and specific. The Holy Spirit speaks clearly to His messenger to reveal exactly what kind of a response is needed. God will show how to call for that response, as well. This is part of the benefit of being a Spirit-baptized minister!

> *The preacher must listen to the voice of the Holy Spirit in order to know what to do.*

God can move in more than one person at a time. On the Day of Pentecost, the Spirit led Peter to call everyone boldly to repent in public. Then the Spirit-baptized preacher became aware of how to cooperate with the conviction of the Spirit in the listeners' hearts. The Holy Spirit was working powerfully in the hearts of thousands of people at the same time:

> *With many other words he warned them;*
> *and he pleaded with them,*
> *"Save yourselves from this corrupt generation."*
> *Those who accepted his message were baptized,*
> *and about three thousand were added to their number that day*
> *(Acts 2:40-41).*

Peter was the first gospel preacher in church history to experience the amazing empowerment of the Holy Spirit in his preaching. God was working in the messenger, in the message, in the call, in the hearers, and in the response — all at the same time! This preaching was not natural, but supernatural.

The Results of Pentecostal Preaching

The result was a miracle of new spiritual birth. Three thousand people who had come to Jerusalem "condemned already" (John 3:18) repented, were forgiven, were brought into new life with Jesus Christ, and received the gift of the Holy Spirit (Acts 2:38).

Like Peter, we must receive power for Pentecostal preaching. Our methods may vary, but our message must be the unchanging gospel. We must clearly display the power of the baptism of the Holy Spirit helping us.

No one should think he or she is unable to receive this gift from God. In his sermon, Peter declared:

> *Repent and be baptized, every one of you...*
> *And you will receive the gift of the Holy Spirit.*
> *The promise is for you and your children*
> *and for all who are far off —*
> *for all whom the Lord our God will call*
> *(Acts 2:38a, 39).*

Only God can give us His power. There is no way to have this level of lasting spiritual impact without using the gift of the Holy Spirit; there is no substitute. Any believer who desires may receive the gift because God specifically offered it to all.

If we try to minister without Christ's gift, we may do some good at times, but we will never complete Christ's commission. The book of Acts teaches that those who work in the mission of God urgently need to be baptized with the Holy Spirit!

The Pattern of Missionary Witness and Discipleship

The book of Acts moves quickly on from the account of the Day of Pentecost. Luke, the author of the book of Acts, was a Gentile. He was careful to show the Gentile expansion of the church in response to the *Missio Dei*. God's Spirit led the way in urging the early church to reach beyond its cultural boundaries with the gospel!

Philip and the Ethiopian Eunuch

In Acts 8, Philip proclaimed the gospel in Samaria after being driven from Jerusalem by persecution. His outreach to the half-Jewish Samaritans was so effective that Peter and John came down to investigate. Both salvation and the baptism of the Holy Spirit were given to this non-Jewish group of believers:

> *When they arrived, they prayed for them*
> *that they might receive the Holy Spirit,*
> *because the Holy Spirit had not yet come upon any of them;*
> *they had simply been baptized into the name of the Lord Jesus.*

> *Then Peter and John placed their hands on them,*
> *and they received the Holy Spirit*
> *(Acts 8:15-17).*

Later, God sent an angel to instruct Philip to leave the revival at Samaria on an unusual mission:

> *"Go south to the road — the desert road —*
> *that goes down from Jerusalem to Gaza."*
> *So he started out, and on his way he met an Ethiopian eunuch,*
> *an important official in charge of all the treasury*
> *of Candace, queen of the Ethiopians.*
> *This man had gone to Jerusalem to worship,*
> *and on his way home was sitting in his chariot*
> *reading the book of Isaiah the prophet.*
> *The Spirit told Philip,*
> *"Go to that chariot and stay near it"*
> *(Acts 8:26b-29).*

Philip had been baptized with the Holy Spirit, and God was able to lead him in very specific ways. It seems unusual for a preacher to leave a powerful revival in town in order to walk in a desert. However, when Philip received these instructions from the Lord, he simply obeyed.

When he saw a foreign chariot being driven to the south, he sensed the Holy Spirit telling him to walk near it. His sensitivity to the Spirit led to the first detailed story of an intercultural witnessing encounter in the book of Acts.

The man in the chariot was an African who had come to Jerusalem to worship God! Probably he had prayed at the Court of the Gentiles that Jesus had cleansed so it would be available for Gentile prayers.

Now he was on his long journey back to the upper region of the Nile. This Ethiopian had purchased a scroll of the prophet Isaiah and was filling his travel time by reading it. For all of his interest in God, he had not yet found salvation on his journey. The Holy Spirit had alerted Philip to find him before it was too late.

> *Then Philip ran up to the chariot*
> *and heard the man reading Isaiah the prophet.*
> *"Do you understand what you are reading?" Philip asked.*
> *"How can I," he said, "unless someone explains it to me?"*
> *So he invited Philip to come up and sit with him*
> *(Acts 8:30-31).*

People around the world are still facing this man's dilemma. How can they understand the Word of God if no one comes to explain it to them? Some modern Ethiopians are still asking this same question today!

> *The eunuch was reading this passage of Scripture:*
> *"He was led like a sheep to the slaughter...*
> *Who can speak of his descendants?*
> *For his life was taken from the earth."*
>
> *...Then Philip began with that very passage of Scripture*
> *and told him the good news about Jesus.*
> *As they traveled along the road, they came to some water*
> *and the eunuch said, "Look, here is water.*
> *Why shouldn't I be baptized?" And he gave orders to stop the chariot.*
> *Then both Philip and the eunuch went down into the water*
> *and Philip baptized him...*
>
> *the Spirit of the Lord suddenly took Philip away,*
> *and the eunuch did not see him again,*
> *but went on his way rejoicing*
> *(Acts 8:32a, 33b, 35-38, 39b).*

God had arranged for Philip to locate the Ethiopian eunuch at the precise moment when he was reading the messianic prophecy of Isaiah 53. Perhaps the eunuch, who could have no children, felt a special kinship with the One described in the prophecy. The mysterious man in the prophecy had no descendants because he had been led like a lamb to the slaughter. How the eunuch longed to know what the passage meant!

The God of all the earth saw the eunuch's spiritual hunger and sent a Spirit-filled messenger to lead him to salvation. It is not possible to overstate the dramatic involvement of the Holy Spirit in this true missionary story.

God's miraculous intervention is obvious in the preparation of the eunuch's heart, the calling of Philip, the prophecy from Isaiah, the timing of the meeting, the eunuch's decision to believe, the sudden discovery of water in the desert, the supernatural transportation of Philip from the scene, and the great joy of the eunuch as he continued on his way home. God had arranged for the gospel to enter Africa!

The Ethiopian eunuch was a sinner in need of salvation; however, he also seems to have been looking sincerely for God. Some people question whether it is "fair" for God to condemn to hell a "sincere seeker" who has never heard the gospel.

Such people are using a human argument which takes no account of the sinfulness of mankind or the holiness of God. All people are sinners. God does not owe salvation to anyone. However, the story of the Ethiopian eunuch gives us great hope for sinners who are sincerely seeking for God.

> *God does not give a burden or calling to His children without a reason.*

God, Who sees the hearts of all people, knows when there is someone who is honestly searching for Him. Acts 8 shows us that God is willing to do extraordinary miracles to bring a gospel messenger to such people. However, the messengers need to be sensitive and obedient to the Holy Spirit!

Philip's experience of divine direction in cross-cultural witness is not meant to be unusual, but normative. The church must send workers wherever the Spirit leads. God does not give a burden or calling to His children without a reason.

The Discipleship Process of Barnabas and Paul

The whole book of Acts describes the advancement of the *Missio Dei*. The later chapters focus on the life of the apostle Paul. The story of how Paul became a missionary gives guidance to the Church in its mission.

To understand the missionary work of Paul, you must know the story of missionary discipleship at the church at Antioch.

> *Now those who had been scattered by the persecution…*
> *traveled as far as Phoenicia, Cyprus, and Antioch,*
> *telling the message only to Jews.*
> *Some of them, however,*
> *men from Cyprus and Cyrene,*
> *went to Antioch and began to speak to Greeks also,*
> *telling them the good news about the Lord Jesus.*
> *The Lord's hand was with them,*
> *and a great number of people believed and turned to the Lord…*
> *(Acts 11:19-21).*

At first the disciples tended to tell the gospel only to people from their own culture; however, the Spirit soon led them across the Jewish cultural barrier. God used Jewish believers from the Mediterranean island of Cyprus and the North African port city of Cyrene to witness to Gentiles in Antioch.

Antioch was the third largest city in the Roman Empire. It was the kind of place that was important to business, but that a strict Jew might want to avoid. It was a Gentile city, filled with pagan people and their false gods.

God did not avoid the strategic city of Antioch; instead, He sent believers to preach there. Just as promised in the Great Commission, "The Lord's hand was with them" (Acts 11:21a). The gospel spread out of this important central city. Many Gentiles were saved at Antioch!

God's plan was not for people simply to be converted but also to become part of local churches. In these groups of believers, God's grace could flow between all the members. Here the strategic work of discipleship of new believers could take place.

> *News of this reached the ears of the church at Jerusalem,*
> *and they sent Barnabas to Antioch.*
> *When he arrived and saw the evidence of the grace of God,*
> *he was glad and encouraged them all*
> *to remain true to the Lord with all their hearts.*
> *He was a good man, full of the Holy Spirit and faith,*
> *and a great number of people were brought to the Lord*
> *(Acts 11:22-23).*

Barnabas is a wonderful example of a person committed to the work of establishing new converts as disciples. Jesus had said to make disciples of all nations. Barnabas was perhaps the first Christian to devote himself full-time to international discipleship. Certainly, he and the church in Antioch were Great Commission pioneers.

When Barnabas came to the Gentile believers in Antioch, he saw God's grace in them and he was glad! A generous spirit is a necessity in someone who wants to make disciples. Barnabas encouraged the new believers. He stayed with them to give an example of Christian living. He showed them how to remain true to the Lord with all their hearts.

It took a good man, full of faith and full of the Holy Spirit, to do such a work. May God call thousands of new "Barnabas International Disciplemakers" around the world! There are not nearly enough of them!

> *Then Barnabas went to Tarsus to look for Saul,*
> *and when he found him, he brought him to Antioch.*
> *So for a whole year Barnabas and Saul met with the church*
> *and taught great numbers of people.*
> *The disciples were called Christians first at Antioch*
> *(Acts 11:25-26).*

Barnabas not only gave himself to the work of discipling new converts but also dedicated much time and energy to discipling new workers. If Barnabas had not believed in Saul when others doubted him, perhaps Saul would never have become a worker in the church.

Barnabas, the disciple-maker, helped Saul find a new identity as a worker in God's mission. Without the disciple-maker Barnabas, there would never have been a missionary Paul!

Without the disciple-maker Barnabas, there would never have been a missionary Paul!

Barnabas was busy in the work of disciple making and in helping lost Gentiles in Antioch to become disciples. There was much work to do because many people had been saved. Barnabas could not do it all. He needed more workers; so he went to find Saul and formed a ministry team with him in Antioch.

Later, when Saul was established as a co-worker and a very successful disciple maker, Barnabas helped him to become a teacher and a leader. At this point, Saul's identity changed and he became Paul the missionary. Paul also became the leader of the team. Barnabas graciously made room for the leadership gifts God had given to Paul.

Finally, Paul formed his own team and began to address the task of worker development and leadership training on their own.

Applying the New Testament Process of Discipleship Today

Barnabas had a good understanding of the ministry of discipleship. I believe that he served as a gatekeeper who allowed Paul access to the future ministry to which he was called. The task of making room for and equipping new workers is at the heart of biblical mentoring and discipleship. Saul/Paul is a good example of the biblical model of discipleship and leader development. As God moved in his life, Paul progressed along the following stages:

The Progression of New Testament Discipleship			
STAGE in the DISCIPLESHIP PROCESS:	EXAMPLE in the CHURCH (and in the Bible):	GOAL: (the Work of the Disciple at this stage)	KEY QUESTION: (the job that only This person can do)
PRE-DISCIPLE	*Unsaved Person* (Saul, the Pharisee)	To Receive Salvation	"What will I do with Jesus?"
DISCIPLE	*New Convert* (Saul, the New Believer)	To Be a Disciple	"How can I be like Jesus?"
DISCIPLE MAKER	*Church Worker* (Saul, the Assistant/ co-worker of Barnabas)	To Make Disciples	"How can I help my disciples to be more like Jesus?"
LEADER WHO DEVELOPS NEW DISCIPLE MAKERS	*Church Leader* (Paul, the Teacher, Missionary, and Apostle)	To Develop Workers	"How can I help my workers to make disciples?"

Figure 9.1

Barnabas participated in bringing Paul through this process and your writer believes he encouraged Paul to pass the process on to others. Later in the book of Acts, Paul helped people such as Silas, Titus, and Timothy to grow through the same stages, until they also became new leaders who could develop workers of their own. Late in his life, Paul exhorted Timothy to also pass on this process.

> *And the things you have heard **me** say*
> *in the presence of many witnesses*
> *[**you** must] entrust to **reliable men***
> *who will also be qualified to teach **others***
> *(2 Timothy 2:2; emphasis mine).*

Note that the four stages are present in Paul's command to Timothy:

- "me" (the leader),
- "you" (the worker who is a potential leader),
- "reliable men" (the disciples who are potential workers),
- and "others (the pre-disciples who are potential disciples of Jesus).

The table shows how important each stage of discipleship is. If "pre-disciples" are not being evangelized by the disciples, the church will not grow. If new converts are not discipled, few of their unsaved friends will be evangelized. If new workers are not being trained, there will be no one to make the new disciples. If leaders do not develop new workers, there will not be enough workers to disciple the new converts.

Notice also that if a leader does not invite mature workers to share the work of leadership with him or her, that leader will not be able to train enough workers for a growing church. If the leader does not develop new leaders to stand with him or her in the work, the leader may be able to *add* a few new workers, but will not be able to *multiply* workers. Without *many* new workers, what will become of the converts who need to be discipled? They may fall into discouragement, sin, or error; then the church will become guilty of not making disciples — the very thing we are commissioned to do.

Each stage is vital. If any part is missing, the process of discipleship will come to a halt. Sadly, in many churches the task of making disciples happens only accidentally, or not at all.

The goal of successful ministers is to give the ministry away!

The goal of successful ministers is not to hold on to the ministry for themselves. Instead, they always are working to give the ministry away to as many new workers and leaders as possible! They disciple others well so that these people can take their place in the *Missio Dei*. This is the Holy Spirit's plan for growing the church!

The Missionary Cycle in Acts

After Barnabas and Paul had spent some time making new disciples and workers in Antioch, God called them to duplicate this ministry in other places and cultures, as well. Now cross-cultural missions would begin in earnest.

> *In the church at Antioch there were prophets and teachers:*
> *Barnabas, Simeon called Niger, Lucius of Cyrene, Manaen...and Saul.*
> *While they were worshiping the Lord and fasting,*
> *the Holy Spirit said, "Set apart for me Barnabas and Saul*
> *for the work to which I have called them."*
> *So after they had fasted and prayed,*
> *they placed their hands on them and sent them off.*
> *The two of them, sent on their way by the Holy Spirit,*
> *went down to Seleucia and sailed from there...*
> *(Acts 13:1-4).*

The church at Antioch was strengthened by its Spirit-led leadership and active discipleship ministry. It continued to grow in numbers and in spiritual maturity. Since it was a Pentecostal church, its leaders were open to messages of prophecy.

God told the church to take two of its very best leaders and set them apart for intercultural ministry in places that had never heard the gospel. Paul's first missionary journey had begun.

The pages that follow are filled with challenges and with the overcoming power of God. Paul and Barnabas established churches in many cities in Cyprus and Asia Minor, and many Gentiles believed. Once Paul was stoned and left for dead, but God revived him when the local disciples prayed (Acts 14:19-20). Making disciples is important. Your disciple's prayers may save your life!

Completing the Missionary Cycle

Paul and Barnabas did not stay in their new mission field permanently. Since they were accountable to the church that sent them, they returned to bring back the story of what God had done.

> *From Attalia they sailed back to Antioch,*
> *where they had been committed to the grace of God*
> *for the work they had now completed.*
> *On arriving there, they gathered the church together*
> *and reported all that God had done through them*
> *and how he had opened the door of faith to the Gentiles.*
> *And they stayed there a long time with the disciples*
> *(Acts 14:26-28).*

The end of the first missionary journey teaches us something very important. Paul and Barnabas returned back to their sending church in Antioch. In spite of all their travels and experiences, they were still accountable to report to the home body that sent them out under the leading of the Holy Spirit.

When they arrived back in Antioch, they told the stories of all that God had done. The home church rejoiced! It was encouraged to send out more missionaries in the future. Paul and Barnabas were given opportunity to minister and to be refreshed. Soon God would send them out again.

The Missionary Cycle Today

The God who called Barnabas and Paul from Antioch will also call workers and leaders to go as cross-cultural missionaries today. No church that understands the *Missio Dei* will resist when God asks for it to send its own messengers to unsaved people in other places. This is part of the glory of being the church of Jesus Christ. After all, Jesus Himself crossed the barrier from heaven to earth to bring Good News to us!

Churches need to send missionaries to be healthy. In addition, they need to hear reports of the impact these workers are having in the places where

God has called them. What a great joy to realize that we have the dignity in our own church to partner with the Mission of God!

Missionaries need to be willing to return home to tell the story to those who sent them. The message that reaches from the church to the lost is not complete until the progress of that message is reported back to the home church.

Good news of the gospel goes from the church to the nations. When the people of the nations believe and become disciples, the good news of eleventh-hour harvest needs to return to the churches. Perhaps more potential eleventh-hour laborers are standing there idle, without a significant purpose for their lives, waiting for a calling! When they hear the report, they too may feel called into the eleventh-hour harvest.

The nations need to hear the gospel, and the churches need to hear the ongoing report of the expansion of the Kingdom of God. It was after Paul and Barnabas told their missionary stories to the Antioch church that a new generation of missionaries, Silas and John Mark, responded or committed themselves to their own missionary callings.

The book of Acts says that Paul and Barnabas eventually parted over a quarrel (15:39). Barnabas wanted to disciple another young worker, John Mark. However, Paul did not want to invest in John Mark again, since he had deserted them on the first missionary journey. Barnabas and Mark went one way, while Paul and Silas went another. However, at the end of his life, Paul says that John Mark had in fact become an important helper to him in the ministry (2 Timothy 4:11). Barnabas' anointed and merciful discipleship ministry seems to have succeeded with John Mark in the end.

Paul's Missionary Ministry

As the apostle Paul matured into a mighty man of God, he never forgot that he was called to be a missionary to the nations.

> *Paul, a servant of Christ Jesus,*
> *called to be an apostle and set apart for the gospel of God...*
> **we received grace and apostleship**
> **to call people from among all the Gentiles**
> **to the obedience that comes from faith**
> *(Romans 1:1, 5b; emphasis mine).*

Paul's ministry goal was to disciple the Gentiles; however, this focus on Gentiles was not appreciated by many of the Jews whom he encountered:

> *On the next Sabbath almost the whole city [of Pisidian Antioch] gathered*
> *to hear the word of the Lord.*
> *When the Jews saw the crowds, they were filled with jealousy*
> *and talked abusively against what Paul was saying.*
> *Then Paul and Barnabas answered them boldly:*
> *"We had to speak the word of God to you first.*
> *Since you reject it and do not consider yourselves worthy of eternal life,*
> *we now turn to the Gentiles.*
> ***For this is what the Lord has commanded us:***
> ***"I have made you a light for the Gentiles,***
> ***that you may bring salvation to the ends of the earth.""***
> *When the Gentiles heard this,*
> *they were glad and honored the word of the Lord;*
> *and all who were appointed for eternal life believed*
> *(Acts 13:44-48; emphasis mine).*

Paul consistently preached the gospel to Gentiles who did not understand the Jewish culture in which Paul had been trained as a Pharisee. He was willing to cross the bridge of culture to evangelize them. So many Gentiles were converted that a special church council was held in Jerusalem to deal with the issue of Gentile believers (Acts 15). This was the meeting where James quoted the prophecy of Amos and applied it to the current issue of non-Jewish converts:

> *Brothers, listen to me.*
> *Simon has described to us how God at first showed his concern*
> *by taking from the Gentiles a people for himself.*
> *The words of the prophets are in agreement with this, as it is written:*
> *'After this I will return and rebuild David's fallen tent...*
> *that the remnant of men may seek the Lord,*
> *and all the Gentiles who bear my name,'*
> *says the Lord, who does these things.*
>
> *...It is my judgment, therefore, that we should not make it difficult*
> *for the Gentiles who are turning to God...*
> *(Acts 15:13b-15a, 16a, 17, 19)*

Paul continued to reach out to "all the Gentiles who bear my name." He trained up fellow workers such as Timothy and Titus, just as Barnabas had trained him to do.

Missionary Case Study: The Gospel Arrives in Europe

By listening to the Holy Spirit, Paul became the first person recorded in Scripture to bring the gospel to Europe. Through a dream, God called him to evangelize a place in the modern-day Balkans (southeastern Europe):

> *...they tried to enter Bithynia, but the Spirit of Jesus*
> *would not allow them to...*
> *During the night Paul had a vision of a man of Macedonia*
> *standing and begging him, 'Come over to Macedonia and help us.'*
> *...we got ready at once to leave for Macedonia,*
> *concluding that God had called us to preach the gospel to them.*
> *...we traveled to Philippi, a Roman colony*
> *and the leading city of that district of Macedonia.*
> *And we stayed there several days*
> *(Acts 16:7b, 9, 10b, 12).*

There was no Jewish prayer building in Philippi where Paul could preach. However, since Paul's God was King of all the earth, no building was required for preaching. Paul adapted his ministry plan for the sake of the Gentiles that he had been sent to reach.

> *On the Sabbath we went outside the city gate to the river,*
> *where we expected to find a place of prayer.*
> *We sat down and began to speak to the women who had gathered there.*
> *One of those listening was a woman named Lydia,*
> *a dealer in purple cloth from the city of Thyatira...*
> *The Lord opened her heart to respond to Paul's message.*
> *When she and the members of her household were baptized,*
> *she invited us to her home...*
> *(Acts 16:13-15a).*

By adapting to the prayer patterns of the unsaved Macedonian people, Paul and his missionary team found Gentile hearers for their message.

The team must have felt strange to pray outside on the banks of a river, in a foreign continent, surrounded by Gentile women and their servants. However, the setting was not strange for God. He had already come to the city by the river long before, preparing the heart of a rich merchant lady named Lydia.

Paul did not see thousands saved on that day, as Peter had at Pentecost. However, the Holy Spirit was no less present. The Spirit was working in Paul as he spoke and in Lydia as she listened. By sensing the Holy Spirit's work in this strange place and cooperating with it, Paul was able to lead Lydia and her entire household to the Lord.

Once they believed, they were baptized. Those in Lydia's household were now full members in the body of Christ, even though they were not Jewish at all. As new converts, they were candidates for Christian discipleship. The first church in Europe had begun!

Paul and his team stayed at Lydia's house, beginning the all-important work of new convert discipleship and winning others to Christ. Before the team's ministry in Philippi was finished, the new missionary church would become a very interesting mix of people.

There was the upper class household of Lydia. There was a formerly demon-possessed slave girl who had been delivered in the public market. After Paul and Silas were thrown into jail, a tough Roman jailer and his household were added to the church, as well.

Paul's Ongoing Discipleship of the First European Church

Imagine the different cultures in the church at Philippi! There were people involved in business, in labor, and in government. There were successful merchants, lowly slaves, and former Roman soldiers (the jailer). Very few were Jewish, but all now belonged to Jesus. After Paul and his team left, this diverse congregation had to learn how to work together with love and respect. No wonder Paul later wrote a missionary letter to this church:

I thank my God every time I remember you.
In all my prayers for all of you, I always pray with joy
because of your partnership in the gospel from the first day until now,
being confident of this,
that he who began a good work in you
will carry it on to completion until the day of Christ Jesus.
It is right for me to feel this way about all of you, since I have you in my heart...

...make my joy complete by being like minded,
having the same love,
being one in spirit and purpose...
Each of you should look not only to your own interests,
but also to the interests of others...

continue to work out your salvation with fear and trembling,
for it is God who works in you to will and to act according to his good purpose.
Do everything without complaining or arguing,
so that you may become blameless and pure, children of God...
(Philippians 1:3-7a, 2:2, 4, 12b-15a).

Paul's letter to the Philippians is a window into the nature of his mission work. We can see his loving attitude in his ministry. Paul was not afraid to give the new believers very specific and practical words of counsel. He also was not afraid to show his deep love for believers in the Philippian church.

Paul clearly remembered "the first day" when the church was born on the banks of the river. He also knew the great variety of people in the church. He knew that such a diverse group could have difficulty in getting along.

Paul's words of love are mixed with encouragement for the Philippians to live in unity and to consider each others' needs. All of this was to be done in the sight of a watchful, omnipresent God. Paul knew that the Holy Spirit was powerfully at work in the lives of these Gentile people in their distant city!

Summary

The book of Acts and the New Testament letters tell the story of the expansion of the *Missio Dei* in the power of the Spirit. The ability to fulfill God's mission comes by divine empowerment which God gives through the baptism of the Holy Spirit. The New Testament shows us the dynamics of Holy Spirit involvement in preaching, calling people to spiritual response, witnessing, and discipleship. Missionary discipleship includes the mentoring of new converts, church workers, and new leaders who will train more workers.

Review and Application

Now that you have completed your study of God's mission as it is narrated in the book of Acts, I pray that you will seek to apply the principles you have studied in your own ministry.

1. Jesus did not want his followers to take up God's mission before they had been filled with God's power. How did the empowerment of the church take place?

2. Explain the points in the content of the apostles' preaching (*kerygma*). Why is each of the points important? Have you ever preached a sermon using the apostles' "outline"?

3. Tell the story of the first conversion of an African recorded in Scripture. What is miraculous about the story? What power accomplished these miracles?

4. What are the four stages of Barnabas' and Paul's discipleship process? What is the special job for each stage that only the person at that stage can do?

5. Discuss the importance of each stage of the "missionary cycle." Why is it important that the church be involved in sending and helping missionaries?

6. How can you be involved in continuing the story of the *Missio Dei*?

Be prepared to discuss these questions and any other questions or issues that come to mind when your instructor refers to them in class.

God's Mission Illustrated in the Missionary Letters

*T*he *epistles* of the New Testament were real letters written in response to actual situations (events) in the missionary church plants. This is why they are sometimes called "situational epistles."

It is common to call these letters *pastoral epistles* (letters written to pastors), or *general epistles* (letters written to churches and individuals). It is more accurate to call them *missionary letters*, written to missionary church plants (new churches that have been established or "planted") and the missionary associates who led them (York, 90).

The Purpose of the New Testament Letters

The New Testament epistles are memos from the living laboratory of missionary church planting — each one addressed a practical situation. The epistles are also windows on how the church today is to go about fulfilling the *Missio Dei!*

Practical Situations in the Newly Planted Churches

Paul's letters read like discipleship guides for the church to follow. Sometimes they celebrated the blessings of a healthy, growing church. To the church at Philippi he wrote, "Therefore, my brothers, you whom I love and long for, my joy and my crown, that is how you should stand firm in the Lord, dear friends!" (Philippians 4:1).

> *The New Testament epistles are memos from the living laboratory of missionary church planting.*

Not every church was as healthy as the congregation at Philippi. Serious problems arose in places such as Corinth. For instance, one letter addressed a practical question about marriage from an earlier letter that the church had sent to him:

> *Now for the matters you [believers in Corinth] wrote about:*
> *It is good for a man not to marry. But since there is so much immorality,*
> *each man should have his own wife, and each woman her own husband*
> *(1 Corinthians 7:1-2).*

Real people have real problems. Regardless of what the issue is, God has wisdom to help His people. Disciples may need teaching to understand the practical wisdom in the Word of God. They also need exhortation to obey those teachings!

At other times, Paul wrote to correct problems in a missionary church plant. Paul could not travel back to Corinth; so he wrote to the Corinthians to correct a problem in their communion service. Paul went to extra effort to disciple these believers.

> *In the following directives I have no praise for you*
> *[believers in Corinthian church],*
> *for your meetings do more harm than good…*
> *as you eat, each of you goes ahead without waiting for anybody else.*
> *One remains hungry, another gets drunk.*

> *Don't you have homes to eat and drink in?*
> *...so then, my brothers, when you come together to eat, wait for each other.*
> *If anyone is hungry, he should eat at home,*
> *so that when you meet together it may not result in judgment.*
> *And when I come I will give further directions*
> *(1 Corinthians 11:17, 21-22a, 33-34).*

The job of teaching believers how they are to serve God, and how they are to behave as God's children, involves much attention to detail. The man or woman of God must be able to exhort the disciples as to how they should act in their new Christian lives.

Paul also sent rebukes to churches that were straying away from the true grace of God into legal religion or false doctrine. Such was the case in Galatia:

> *I am astonished that you [churches in Galatia] are so quickly deserting*
> *the one who called you by the grace of Christ*
> *and are turning to a different gospel — which is really no gospel at all...*
> *Did you receive the Spirit by observing the law,*
> *or by believing what you heard?*
> *Are you so foolish?*
> *After beginning with the Spirit,*
> *are you now trying to attain your goal by human effort?*
> *(Galatians 1:6-7a, 3:2b-3).*

New believers may become confused if they are left without discipleship for too long a time. Paul had to write urgently to them to remind them of what they had believed when they were saved.

Paul also wrote letters asking for the churches he had planted to be involved in serious missionary prayers for his own work. He needed Holy Spirit empowerment and courage. He wanted the Holy Spirit to provide him with words to speak, and he was not ashamed to ask for the people of a church plant to pray for him. Look at his appeal to the believers in the church plant at Ephesus:

> *Pray also for me, that whenever I open my mouth*
> *words may be given me*
> *so that I will fearlessly make known the mystery of the gospel,*
> *for which I am an ambassador in chains.*
> *Pray that I may declare it fearlessly, as I should*
> *(Ephesians 6:19-20).*

Paul knew that the prayers of the believers were essential to the forward progress of the Mission of God. Are we praying about the *Missio Dei* in our churches and classes?

A Far-Reaching Effort

Paul planted churches in the Mediterranean islands, in Asia Minor (Turkey), in eastern Europe, and perhaps even as far as Spain. As a mature missionary and apostle, Paul could write to the Romans:

> *I have written you quite boldly on some points,*
> *as if to remind you of them again,*
> *because of the grace God gave me*
> *to be a minister of Christ Jesus to the Gentiles*
> *with the priestly duty of proclaiming the gospel of God,*
> *so that the Gentiles might become an offering acceptable to God,*
> *sanctified by the Holy Spirit*
> *(Romans 15:15-16).*

Paul's greatest ministry satisfaction came from his discipleship of Gentile converts. He was delighted to hear that his disciples were faithful in serving the one true God. He reminded the Romans of "what Christ has accomplished through me in leading the Gentiles to obey God by what I have said and done" (Romans 15:18b). The effective force behind Paul's ministry to the Gentiles was not his status, his personal ability, or his education. He accomplished this great work by the power of signs and miracles, through the power of the Spirit (Romans 15:19a).

Paul had a relentless drive to bring the gospel to new places. The condition of the totally unreached compelled him to keep moving forward:

> *So from Jerusalem all the way around to Illyricum*
> [that is, from Israel/Palestine to the Macedonia/Bosnia region],
> *I have fully proclaimed the gospel of Christ.*
> *It has always been my ambition to preach the gospel*
> *where Christ was not known...*
> *(Romans 15:19b-20a).*

It is amazing to look on a map and see how far away Paul traveled in spreading the gospel. He ministered extensively in lands now part of the modern day nations of Israel, Syria, Turkey, Bosnia/Macedonia, Greece, Italy, Malta, Cyprus, and Crete. According to Romans 15:24, he may have preached as far away as Spain!

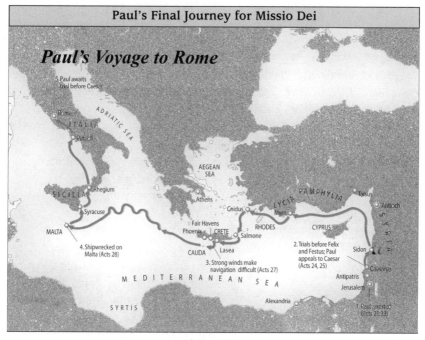

Figure 10.1

Since Paul did not always stay long in a place where he left a new church, the new church needed long-term workers and pastors. Paul often would leave one of his ministers-in-training at a church to establish it while he pushed farther ahead:

> *The reason I left you* [Titus] *in Crete*
> *was that you might straighten out what was left unfinished*
> *and appoint elders in every town, as I directed you*
> *(Titus 1:5).*

Paul had on ongoing ministry of discipling these new leaders that he had left behind. He cared very much for them and tried to visit them and answer their ministry questions. Sometimes they needed encouragement not to give up on a difficult assignment.

> *As I urged you* [Timothy] *when I went into Macedonia,*
> *stay there in Ephesus*
> *so that you may command certain men*
> *not to teach false doctrines any longer...*
> *(1 Timothy 1:3).*

He often wrote letters telling the churches to be responsive to his younger coworkers. In this way, Paul was encouraging their development from disciple-making workers into leaders in their own right.

> *If Timothy comes,*
> *see to it that he has nothing to fear while he is with you* [Corinthians],
> *for he is carrying out the work of the Lord, just as I am.*
> *No one, then, should refuse to accept him.*
> *(1 Corinthians 16:10-11a)*

Paul's work of discipling new workers and leaders created the capacity to disciple the new Gentile converts.

In spite of his great concern for the unsaved, Paul knew that the most important thing he could do was to train up leaders for the new converts to follow. Paul could not do all that he was called to do alone. To do more work, there must be more workers.

Paul's work of discipling new workers and leaders created the capacity to disciple the new Gentile converts. On one occasion, new convert evangelism had to wait while Paul made sure of what was happening to one of his ministers-in-training:

> *Now when I went to Troas to preach the gospel of Christ*
> *and found that the Lord had opened a door for me,*
> *I still had no peace of mind,*
> *because I did not find my brother Titus there.*
> *So I said good-by to them and went on…*
> *(2 Corinthians 2:12-13)*

Since the new converts could not be discipled without a worker, he continued onward.

Paul may have refused to evangelize Troas because there was no long-term worker ready to pastor there. Since his own priority was to connect with Titus, and since the new converts could not be discipled without a worker, he continued onward

At the very end of his life Paul was imprisoned in a Roman jail, awaiting his own execution. It was a close personal relationship with one of his minister-in-training disciples that comforted and inspired Paul at this critical time.

> *Paul, an apostle of Christ Jesus…*
> *To Timothy, my dear son…*
> *I thank God…as night and day I constantly remember you in my prayers.*
> *Recalling your tears, I long to see you, so that I may be filled with joy.*
> *I have been reminded of your sincere faith…*
> *For this reason I remind you to fan into flame the gift of God…*
>
> *Do your best to come to me quickly…*
> *When you come, bring the cloak…and my scrolls…*
> *Only Luke is with me. Get Mark and bring him with you…*
>
> *The Lord will rescue me from every evil attack*
> *and will bring me safely to his heavenly kingdom.*
> *To him be glory for ever and ever.*
> *(2 Timothy 1:1a, 2a, 3b-5a, 6a, 4:9, 11, 13, 18).*

The love and mutual benefit of this discipleship relationship gave Paul comfort and purpose in his last days. No doubt Satan tried to tell Paul that his time in prison was wasted for the ministry, but this was not true. Paul's disciples were still faithfully doing the work he had entrusted to them. Also, while he was in prison Paul wrote many of the letters that have inspired the church for centuries!

God was with Paul to the ends of the earth, and to the end of his life. In his last letter, Paul passed on to Timothy the strategy of the discipleship ministry that he had followed for so many years:

> *You then, my son, be strong in the grace that is in Christ Jesus.*
> *And the things you have heard me say in the presence of many witnesses*
> *entrust to reliable men*
> *who will also be qualified to teach others*
> *(2 Timothy 2:1-2).*

Paul's missionary discipleship strategy involved four groups of people: "me" (the disciple leader), "you" (the worker), "reliable men" (the new disciples), and "others" (the people the new disciples will be teaching tomorrow.)

He had dedicated his life to the ministry of discipling new converts, new workers, and new leaders for the missionary churches. Paul, like Jesus, had greatly multiplied the effect of his ministry by giving the ministry away to well-trained disciples!

Paul himself had gone through this system in his early years as a believer. Barnabas had believed that Paul was a "reliable man" and helped him into the ministry. Later, Paul did the same for Timothy, Titus, Luke, and many others. Now Paul was entrusting his leader-discipleship ministry to Timothy and the next generation.

All ministers of the gospel need to ask themselves if they are continuing on this unbroken chain of discipleship, or not. Who are the reliable men or women that you are discipling right now? Are you teaching them to disciple others, too?

If you commit to a lifelong ministry of discipleship, your last days will be days of victory, not despair. Like Paul, you can have many disciples to continue the work of the Mission of God when you are gone.

Do not hold on tightly to ministry, titles, or position. Give the ministry away to as many reliable, well-discipled people as possible!

The Missionary Calling

Paul had been called to be an apostle "sent one" in a face-to-face meeting with Jesus Christ on the road to Damascus (Acts 9). He was recognized as an "apostle of Christ" for his role in opening up the Gentile churches. Along with establishing new churches, the first (primary) apostles had an authoritative role in determining the doctrinal teaching of the churches. This was because they were first-hand witnesses of the teachings of Jesus.

Apostles of the Early Church

Many other men and women were later called by God to bring the gospel to the Gentile world. Although they may not have known Jesus during His life on earth, they were also appointed as "apostles" by the churches.

These "secondary apostles" (the group of people called "apostles" in the New Testament who, however, were not part of Christ's twelve original apostles) were sent across cultural barriers to plant churches among the Gentiles. Hundreds or even thousands of these workers managed to impact the entire Roman world within one hundred years. They were bringing the blessing of the *Missio Dei* to the nations!

These secondary apostles could be sent out alone or in teams. Paul greeted two of these apostles in the book of Romans. The name "Junias" is feminine and indicates that this apostle was a woman!

> *Greet Andronicus and Junias, my relatives*
> *who have been in prison with me.*
> *They are outstanding among the apostles,*
> *and they were in Christ before I was*
> *(Romans 16:7).*

Today we normally refer to the church's officially appointed church planting representatives as "missionaries." It seems better to reserve the word "apostle" for the original twelve apostles of Jesus, and to avoid the charge of self-promotion that can come from naming oneself "apostle" as if one too had walked with the Twelve during Jesus' ministry among the Jews.

However, it also seems important to emphasize that today's missionaries should still have gospel-oriented, apostolic callings. They also must still be involved in the primary goal of proclaiming the gospel and planting Christ's church in new cultures and places. It is still necessary for all missionaries to be called by God and to focus their efforts on 'making disciples of every nation." Anyone made in the God's image is capable of hearing His call to missionary work. (I combined the preceding 2 sentences with previous paragraph as Paul indicated).

In one sense, all of God's children are called to fulfill the *Missio Dei*. However, there is still a special and divine calling from God to the full-time missionary work of the church. These messengers need to be recognized, supported, and sent out by the church. A missionary that goes through this process will gain increased spiritual power and integrity for their ministry.

The Meaning of the Word "Missionary"

A *missionary* (what I have described as a "secondary apostle") in the New Testament sense is someone who is *sent* from his or her home church to *cross* a cultural barrier, to *plant* new churches, and to *disciple* converts, workers, and leaders. New Testament missionaries sometimes served on unified missionary teams. These teams divided up certain parts of the overall missionary task between the members.

Christian ministers were often called "servants" (James 1:1; Jude 1:1) or "fellow workers" (Romans 16:9; Philemon 1:1) While all believers were called to witness, not all believers were called "missionaries" (apostles). Some are specially called by God to be "missionaries" and to focus their efforts on making disciples of other people groups and nations. Not everyone will be called to be a full-time missionary; however, anyone made in God's image is capable of hearing His call to missionary work.

The cultural barrier that the missionary crossed was usually from Jew to Gentile or from one ethnic group to another. The mission might involve reaching a different culture in the missionary's own city, or traveling to the ends of the earth!

We can learn from the Acts and the epistles that it is normative for the church to have various categories of mission workers. Like Joshua, we must organize effectively if we are to occupy the land God has set out for us.

Since Christ's twelve apostles knew Jesus face, to face, many churches feel it best to reserve the title of "apostle" for them (and for Paul, who is seen as a special case.) However, these churches may still have "bishops" who serve as local pastors, "servants" who do work such as teaching and administrating in the body, "missionaries" who are sent out from the churches to advance the harvest among the nations, and "fellow workers" who do valuable and necessary kingdom work alongside the churches' appointed missionaries.

New Testament missionary categories often seem to overlap one another. The most important thing is not the job title, but the obedient and willing spirit of the man or woman who does it. If it is God who calls, the missionary should work willingly, as working for the Lord!

The Gospel According to Abraham

Paul's letter to the churches in Galatia (southern Asia Minor, in modern Turkey) may have been the first missionary letter that he wrote. Paul was concerned that the churches planted during his first missionary journey were confused about how to experience salvation in their newfound Christian faith.

Going Back to Abraham

To the Galatians, the simple gospel of Paul seemed too easy to be true. Where were the long lists of difficult duties to earn one's way to heaven? Should Galatians imitate the Jews with their difficult religious rules that were necessary for salvation? Even Galatian Christians had begun to submit to Jewish circumcision to ensure their salvation.

Some scholars believe that the book of Galatians was probably written before the Jerusalem Council (Acts 15) in which this very issue was debated (Full Life Study Bible, 1806-7). Paul wanted to clear away the confusion surrounding what it meant for Gentiles to respond to the gospel.

The Jews causing the confusion were proud of their status as "children of Abraham." So Paul goes back to the faith of Abraham to clear up the confusion. The Galatians were turning away to "a different gospel" (Galatians 1:6), thinking that the religion of Abraham was more valid than the gospel of Paul. Paul tells them the truth — the gospel of Paul and the gospel of

Abraham are the same. There never has been more than one gospel that could make mankind right with God!

> *I am astonished that you are so quickly deserting*
> *the one who called you by the grace of Christ*
> *and are turning away to a different gospel — which is really no gospel at all.*
> *Evidently some people are throwing you into confusion*
> *and are trying to pervert the gospel of Christ.*
> *But even if we or an angel from heaven*
> *should preach a gospel other than the one we preached to you,*
> *let him be eternally condemned!*
> *(Galatians 1:6-8).*

Paul is declaring that God had never changed His mind or introduced any new gospel in His effort to save mankind. God always had just one plan in mind, the salvation of all nations through the redemptive work of Jesus Christ.

Abraham and the Missio Dei

Abraham was a part of this original and unchanging plan, even though he lived before Christ's earthly ministry. Jesus' work on the cross reached back in time to save those who simply placed their faith in God. Paul tells the Galatians that this unchanging faith in God's plan to save all nations (the *Missio Dei*) was nothing less than the "gospel of Abraham!"

> *Are you so foolish? After beginning with the Spirit,*
> *are you now trying to attain your goal by human effort?*
>
> *…Does God give you his Spirit and work miracles among you*
> *because you observe the law,*
> *or because you believe what you heard?*
> *Consider Abraham:*
> *"He believed God, and it was credited to him as righteousness." Understand,*
> *then, that those who believe are children of Abraham.*
> **The Scripture foresaw that God would justify the Gentiles by faith,**
> **and announced the gospel in advance to Abraham:**
> **"All nations will be blessed through you."** *So those who have faith are*
> *blessed along with Abraham, the man of faith*
> *(Galatians 3:3, 5-9; emphasis mine).*

Paul says that the gospel itself was announced in advance to Abraham! In saying this, Paul greatly clarified our understanding of the meaning of the *Missio Dei* for New Testament believers.

Like the early believers in Galatia, we see that we cannot be saved by religious performance. Like Abraham, we are saved simply by faith in God and His unchanging redemptive plan.

Stated another way, Paul is saying that you cannot fully appreciate the saving gospel of Jesus Christ unless you understand God's promise to Abraham in Genesis 12:3. There God said, "… all peoples on earth will be blessed through you."

No wonder this promise to Abraham has been called "the fiery center for the rest of Scripture" (John York, 25)! God's unchanging purpose was to give all peoples of the earth the blessing of salvation through Jesus Christ. Abraham understood this and placed his faith in God.

Paul is telling the Galatians not to give up on the unchanging gospel of Abraham by turning aside into recent Jewish religion and legalism. He later reminds them, "It is for freedom that Christ has set us free. Stand firm, then, and do not let yourself be burdened again by a yoke of slavery" (Galatians 5:1).

> *All who rely on observing the law are under a curse…*
> *Christ redeemed us from the curse of the law*
> *by becoming a curse for us, for it is written:*
> *"Cursed is everyone who is hung on a tree."* [Deuteronomy 21:23]
> *He redeemed us in order that*
> *the blessing given to Abraham* [Genesis 12:3]
> *might come to the Gentiles through Christ Jesus, so that by faith we might*
> *receive the promise of the Spirit*
> *(Galatians 3:10a, 13-14).*

Paul sees himself as a missionary sent by God to make the mystery of God's *Missio Dei* plan known to the Gentiles. Salvation in Christ is the fulfillment of the blessing given to Abraham!

At the end of the time period covered in the Pauline epistles and Acts, Paul is in Roman custody waiting for his case to be heard. The story of the *Missio Dei* in the early church does not have a clear ending. God's mission

God's mission is still continuing.

is still continuing. The story of how God's salvation reaches all nations is still being written today. We have the opportunity to live out our own chapter of the expansion of the *Missio Dei* in the power of the Spirit!

Praise God for the power of the unchanging gospel. This gospel was preached by the apostles, empowered by the Holy Spirit, purchased by the blood of Christ, and proclaimed in advance to Abraham!

Summary

The work and definition of missions can be understood by studying the missionary letters. All of this effort was guided by the Holy Spirit in order to bring the blessing of Abraham to the nations of the earth. The story of the expansion of the church in the New Testament does not have a clear ending point. We are still living out the story of the expansion of the *Missio Dei* in the power of the Spirit!

Review and Application

———————●◄——————

Having completed your study of the manner in which God's Mission is illustrated in the missionary letters, think about the implications of the missionary methodology for your own ministry and Christian service.

1. In what way is the ministry of making disciples necessary before any other ministry in the church can take place?

2. Should a local church be willing to hear the ministry reports of a missionary? Is this a minor issue or a major part of the church's mission?

3. Recall the four distinctives or elements that define a fully appointed "missionary" in New Testament practice. (The first has been included for you.)

    *   sent   <u> by the churches   </u>
    *   crosses   _____
    *   plants   _____
    *   disciples   _____, _____, and _____,

4. What did Paul mean by saying that "the Scripture…announced *the gospel* in advance to Abraham" (Galatians 3:8)?

5. Why did God redeem you, according to Galatians 3:14?

6. Do the people in your home church understand why they have been redeemed? Explain how you can know the answer to this question.

Be prepared to discuss these questions and any other questions or issues that come to mind when your instructor refers to them in class.

CHAPTER 11

God's Mission Accomplished in the Book of Revelation

*T*he unfinished work of the Church Age will not continue forever. Sin and suffering will not always endure. Even the preaching of the gospel throughout the earth will one day come to an end. After this, God's glory will be seen clearly and He will be worshipped joyfully by souls made in His own image and freed by redemption from sin.

John, the last of the authors in the Bible, was given a final revelation of the future to encourage and inform the current activities of the church. The book of Revelation looks prophetically into the future to describe the successful completion of the *Missio Dei* on earth.

Revelation gives us a glimpse of the beginning of that new life and glory in God's presence which will never fade away.

The Purpose of the Apocalypse

The book of Revelation is the final book of the Bible. It is a book of dramatic and symbolic prophecy, complete with terrible final judgments and glorious deliverances for God's people. This type of prophetic literature is called "apocalyptic" writing, and the book of Revelation itself is sometimes known as the "Apocalypse."

Why should Christians be concerned with a book that deals with many events still in the future? One reason to study Revelation is that God gave these visions to John so we could glimpse the completion point of the *Missio Dei* here on Earth. When we see the final results of the mission of God, we will be strengthened to keep working for His kingdom!

For those weary in the struggle of discipling all nations, Revelation gives wonderful encouragement. God's plans will prevail! The devil will be defeated — not just for time, but for all eternity. Evil and pain will be completely and finally separated out from all of God's good creation. Disease and death will disappear. What is perfect will endure without end. For Christians, the best is still to come!

Even if Revelation is difficult to understand, we will be blessed by considering the successful and glorious completion of God's mission on earth.

> *Blessed is the one who reads the words of this prophecy,*
> *and blessed are those who hear it*
> *and take to heart what is written in it,*
> *because the time is near*
> *(Revelation 1:3).*

Those who understand the message of God's final victory may be motivated to take their place in the harvest field.

The book of Revelation is not some kind of Christian "magic charm" or "good luck talisman." The blessing of Revelation is for those who both hear it and take it to heart. To "take it to heart" means to believe that this glimpse of the future is accurate and to live as if it will come true. Good theology should lead to good practice.

The time of the fulfillment of the *Missio Dei* is near. The King of the nations will soon arrive to rule the earth. We will be blessed if He finds us busy working for His mission when He comes.

The owner of the vineyard is urgently looking for laborers to work before the eleventh hour is over. In giving us the dramatic message of the book of Revelation, the owner of the vineyard is going out to the marketplace one final time to see if anyone has not yet been mobilized in the harvest. Those who understand the message of God's final victory may be motivated to take their place in the harvest field.

The Victory of the Kingdom

God is the great King over all the earth; however, Satan and those who follow him have rebelled against the rightful and blessed rule of the King. This rebellion cannot be ignored.

God could simply destroy all mankind; instead, He has chosen to let time pass and work to save some of those whom Satan intends to destroy. That is why the *Missio Dei* is the salvation of people from every nation. God will gain the glory by delivering people of every nation out of the hand of Satan.

The Fulfillment of the Covenant Promises

God has dealt with mankind from the very beginning by using the promises of His covenants. We have seen the history of these covenants in this study. Review the progression of God's covenants with mankind in the following table.

Table of Covenants		
Covenant	**Passage**	**Key Phrase**
Adam and Eve	Genesis 3:15	*"...he will crush Your head"*
Noahic	Genesis 9:15	*"...never again will the waters become a flood to destroy all life."*
Abrahamic	Genesis 12.3	*'...and all the peoples of the earth will be blessed through you."*
Davidic	2 Samuel 7:14	*"Your kingdom will endure forever"*
New Covenant	Jeremiah 31:31--34	*"...write it on their hearts."*

Figure 11.1

When we compare God's covenants to the difficulty of life in the world around us, many questions come to mind. For example, what will happen to God's covenant promises? What will happen to Satan and to evildoers? What is the future of those who put their faith in Christ? These are some of the questions that Revelation answers for us.

It is clear that God will have to act if the sins and problems of this world are to be removed. Mankind cannot make this world perfect by his own efforts, even when aided by the best laws ever written:

> **For if there had been nothing wrong with that first covenant,**
> **no place would have been sought for another.**
> *But God found fault with the people and said:*
> *"The time is coming, declares the Lord*
> *when **I will make a new covenant** with the house of Israel*
> *and with the house of Judah.*
> *It will not be like the covenant I made with their forefathers*
> *when I took them by the hand to lead them out of Egypt,*
> *because they did not remain faithful...*
>
> *This is the covenant I will make with the house of Israel after that time...*
> *I will put my laws in their minds and write them on their hearts.*
> *I will be their God, and they will be my people.*
> *No longer will a man teach his neighbor,*
> *or a man his brother, saying 'Know the Lord,'*
> ***because they all will know me,***
> ***from the least of them to the greatest...***
> *(Hebrews 8:7-9a, 10-11; emphasis mine).*

God will bring about the fulfillment of the promises of His new covenant! It is encouraging to remember that the promise of His presence will be given to all people, whether small or great. Revelation gives us a picture of the fulfillment of these prophecies:

> *The seventh angel sounded his trumpet,*
> *and there were loud voices in heaven, which said:*
> *"The kingdom of the world*
> *has become the kingdom of our Lord and of his Christ,*
> *and he will reign for ever and ever."*

> And the twenty-four elders, who were seated on their thrones before God,
> fell on their faces and worshiped God, saying:
> "We give thanks to you, Lord God Almighty,
> who is and who was,
> because you have taken your great power
> and have begun to reign.
> The nations were angry;
> and your wrath has come.
> The time has come for judging the dead,
> and for rewarding your servants the prophets
> and your saints and those who reverence your name,
> both small and great —
> and for destroying those who destroy the earth" (Revelation 11:15-18).

The small and great of the earth together can trust their case to the judgment of the Almighty God, for His judgments are just and effective. The salvation, the power, and the kingdom of God will triumph until all the people of the world acknowledge the authority of Christ:

> Then I heard a loud voice in heaven say:
> "Now have come **the salvation**
> and **the power**
> and **the kingdom** of our God,
> and **the authority** of his Christ.
> For the accuser of our brothers,
> who accuses them before our God day and night,
> has been hurled down.
> They overcame him by the blood of the Lamb
> and the word of their testimony;
> they did not love their lives so much as to shrink from death.
> Therefore rejoice, you heavens and you who dwell in them!"
> (Revelation 12:10-12a; emphasis mine).

The accuser of the brothers, Satan, will be hurled down by the power of God. God will enable us to overcome the adversary who accuses us before God. Believers in Jesus will overcome by the power of the blood of Christ, and by the faith they show in their testimony! Revelation shows us that Satan's failure is sure: "He is filled with fury, because he knows that his time is short" (Revelation 12:12c).

The Final Judgment and Separation of Souls

Opponents who know they will be defeated may be filled with rage. We may see the signs of Satan's fury, but he is already a defeated foe. All of the deception, all of the sin, and all of the rebellion of human history will be judged. Listen to John's vision of the final end of Satan and his demonic forces:

> *I saw heaven standing open*
> *and there before me was a white horse,*
> *whose rider is called Faithful and True.*
> *With justice he judges and makes war.*
> *His eyes are like blazing fire, and on his head are many crowns…*
> *He treads the winepress of the fury of the wrath of God Almighty.*
> *On his robe and on his thigh he has this name written:*
> *KING OF KINGS AND LORD OF LORDS.*
> *…Then I saw the beast and the kings of the earth and their armies*
> *gathered together to make war against the rider on the horse and his army.*
> *But the beast was captured, and with him the false prophet…*
> *The two of them were thrown alive into the fiery lake of burning sulfur*
> *(Revelation 19:11-12a, 15b-16, 19-20a, 20c).*

There will be no remedy and no return for the devil. At this judgment, Satan's deceptions will be punished eternally.

> *And the devil, who deceived them, was thrown into the lake of burning sulfur,*
> *where the beast and the false prophet had been thrown.*
> *They will be tormented day and night for ever and ever*
> *(Revelation 20:10).*

As the redeemed in heaven view the doom of Satan and his rebellion against God, they will sing a mighty song of praise that will be wonderful to hear. John saw it in his vision and describes it for us:

> *After this I heard what sounded*
> *like the roar of a great multitude in heaven shouting:*
> *"Hallelujah!*
> *Salvation and glory and power belong to our God,*
> *for true and just are his judgments"*
> *(Revelation 19:1-2a).*

God is not just planning to remove evil from the earth; He is creating a new, undefiled heaven and earth. He Himself will dwell in this new creation! God will be immediately present in the "new heaven and new earth."

> *Then I saw a new heaven and a new earth,*
> *for the first heaven and the first earth had passed away...*
> *And I heard a loud voice from the throne saying,*
> *"Now the dwelling of God is with men,*
> *and he will live with them.*
> *They will be his people,*
> *and God himself will be with them*
> *and be their God" (Revelation 21:1a, 3).*

God's presence is what will make heaven great! We will no longer have to instruct one another on how to relate to God, for every person in heaven, from the least to the greatest, will know him intimately.

> *"No longer will a man teach his neighbor,*
> *or a man his brother, saying 'Know the Lord,'*
> *because they will all know me,*
> *from the least of them to the greatest," declares the Lord.*
> *(Jeremiah 31:34).*

In the new world God is preparing, some things will be specifically left out:

> *He will wipe away every tear from their eyes.*
> *There will be no more death or mourning*
> *or crying or pain,*
> *for the old order of things has passed away.*
> *He who was seated on the throne said,*
> *"I am making everything new!"*
> *Then he said, "Write this down,*
> *for these words are trustworthy and true" (Revelation 21:4-5).*

What a comfort to serve the God who is acting to solve all problems that we face. What a joy to be promised that we will know the One Who makes life worthwhile.

God's presence is what will make heaven great!

In God's perspective, the work is already done. He has already promised to satisfy everyone who submits to His kingdom with the blessings of the King. However, those who do not submit to Him will have a different end. There will be a great divide of souls. All mankind will experience one of two destinies.

> *It is done.*
> *I am the Alpha and the Omega, the Beginning and the End.*
> *To him who is thirsty I will give to drink without cost*
> *from the spring of the water of life.*
> *He who overcomes will inherit all this,*
> *and I will be his God and he will be my son.*
> *But the cowardly, the unbelieving, the vile,*
> *the murderers, the sexually immoral,*
> *those who practice magic arts,*
> *the idolaters and all liars —*
> *their place will be in the fiery lake of burning sulfur.*
> *This is the second death*
> *(Revelation 21:6-8).*

Those who overcome Satan's fury now will be satisfied forever with God's living water! In fact, Revelation tells us that God will give us the inheritance and adopt us as His sons.

> *There will be a great divide of souls.*

Those who do not accept God's current mercy will be left out of His Kingdom blessings. The only place left for the unbelievers will be the fiery lake reserved for Satan and his followers. An eternal separation from God in the deserved punishment of hell is their destiny, as John was told: "This is the second death" (Revelation 21:8).

The Blessing for All Nations

The biblical theology of missions teaches that the theme of the entire Bible concerns the nations. God's mission is to redeem people for His name from among all the people groups on earth.

In Revelation, we glimpse the future of this plan. God is creating a new heaven in which we all can live. He plans to bring all nations into this blessed place!

The Living Water

As John wrote the book of Revelation, the Holy Spirit gave him visions of the fulfillment of many biblical themes. One such theme is the giving of living water.

John sees the nations of the world blessed by a wonderful river filled with the water of life: "Then the angel showed me the river of the water of life, as clear as crystal, flowing from the throne of God and of the Lamb" (Revelation 22:1). In God's mercy, the nations that were under the sentence of death from sin are now redeemed and can drink the water of life. What a wonderful hope!

The nations are thirsty for life that only God can provide. God's concern for the nations is a consistent theme in all the writings of John. John portrays Jesus as the Savior of the entire inhabited earth. This phrase is like a song that repeats again and again every time John writes about Jesus. Remember: John had mentioned this theme when he wrote about Jesus' ministry to the woman at the well. There Jesus used the metaphor of living water to search out the faith of that Samaritan woman.

> *Everyone who drinks this water will be thirsty again,*
> *but whoever drinks the water I give him will never thirst.*
> *Indeed the water I give him will become in him*
> *a spring of water welling up to eternal life*
> *(John 4:13).*

When the woman showed how much she longed for eternal life, Jesus clearly revealed to her that He Himself was the Messiah. The woman believed, and her testimony led many of the townspeople to come to Jesus. The final words of these Gentiles who believed in Jesus were insightful: "We know that this man really is the Savior of the world" (John 4:42b).

Many years later, John wrote a letter to the missionary churches under his pastoral care. When John needed to remind the churches of exactly who it is that they were serving, he remembered the words of the Samaritan confession so long ago. To John, there was no better way to describe who Jesus really is:

> *And we have seen and testify*
> *that the Father has sent His Son*
> *to be the Savior of the world*
> *(1 John 4:14).*

The Kingdom of Priests

Another fulfilled theme is that of the "kingdom of priests." Here at the end of God's Word, John begins by rejoicing that we as New Testament believers are part of the fulfillment of God's mission (York, 98).

> *To him who loves us and has freed us from our sins by his blood,*
> *and has made us to **be a kingdom and priests** to serve his God and Father—*
> *to him be glory and power for ever and ever! Amen*
> *(Revelation 1:5b-6; emphasis mine).*

The "kingdom and priests" refers back to Exodus 19:6, when God told His people Israel that they would be a "kingdom of priests" to show His glory to the nations.

This theme was continued in the book of the prophet Zechariah. A figure called "Joshua," representing the whole kingdom of Israel, stood before God to serve as a priest, but he was dressed in filthy robes (Zechariah 3:1-7). Zechariah was declaring that the "kingdom of priests" needed to be cleansed in order to serve the nations.

In the New Testament, the apostle Peter told believers in the church that they had become God's kingdom of priests. The necessary cleansing has now been provided by Christ!

> *But you are a chosen people, a royal priesthood…*
> *that you may declare the praises of him*
> *who called you out of darkness into his wonderful light*
> *(1 Peter 2:9).*

John is reminding us that we who serve the king have a priestly function to bring the nations to relationship with Jesus Christ. In Revelation, God tells us one more time that His concern is for every nation on earth!

> *Look, he is coming with the clouds,*
> *and every eye will see him,*
> *even those who pierced him;*
> *and all the peoples of the earth will mourn*
> *because of him*
> *(Revelation 1:7).*

Every eye will see Him. We who know the Lord will rejoice, but those of every nation who did not know Him will mourn. When He comes, the response of the people of the nations will show to which kingdom they belong.

The Mission of Jesus

When Jesus is revealed as the Lamb that had been slain, the elders of heaven praise Him for His worthiness. In their praise, they reveal that the purpose of Christ's sufferings was to bless all nations:

> *Then I saw a Lamb, looking as if it had been slain,*
> *standing in the center of the throne...*
> *the four living creatures and the twenty-four elders*
> *fell down before the Lamb...*
> *And they sang a new song:*
> *"You are worthy to take the scroll and to open its seals,*
> *because You were slain,*
> *and with Your blood You purchased men for God*
> *from every tribe and language and people and nation.*
> *You have made them to be a kingdom and priests*
> *to serve our God..."*
> *(Revelation 5:6, 8a, 9-10a).*

While the rebellious of the earth suffer the wrath of God, another great multitude is having a different experience in heaven. Listen to the song of the nations who love the Lord:

> *After this I looked*
> *and there before me was a great multitude that no one could count,*
> *from every nation, tribe, people, and language,*
> *standing before the throne and in front of the Lamb...*
> *And they cried out in a loud voice:*
> *"Salvation belongs to our God,*
> *who sits on the throne,*
> *and to the Lamb" (Revelation 7:9-10).*

Every nation, every tribe, every people group, and every language will be represented in heaven. It must be so, for our God is the King of the Nations! The nations in heaven rejoice and sing a song that only the redeemed can sing: *"Salvation belongs to our God"* (Revelation 7:10b).

They do not call him "the God of the Jews," "the God of another culture," or "the God of another race." In heaven, the people of every nation testify that the risen Christ is their very own. He belongs to believers in all of the earth, for He created and saved them all. Like the Samaritans did so long ago, believers of every nation will see Him as their own. They will proclaim: "He is *our* God — and His Kingdom shall never end!"

The New City and its Occupants

Satan is cast down in stages in the book of Revelation. One verse reveals the charges against him. The crime listed against Satan is that he is the one who leads the world astray:

> *The great dragon was hurled down —*
> *that ancient serpent called the devil, or Satan,*
> *who leads the whole world astray*
> *(Revelation 12:9a).*

While Satan is losing his battle to lead the whole world astray, a contrast is taking place in heaven. A choir of saved humanity sings about how the Lamb of God has won the hearts of the world by His righteous acts:

> *Who will not fear you, O Lord,*
> *and bring glory to your name?*
> *For you alone are holy.*
> *All nations will come and worship before you,*
> *for your righteous acts have been revealed*
> *(Revelation 15:4).*

When these transitional times are over, God will remove sin and rebellion from His presence forever. Then a new, undefiled heaven and earth will come down from God.

> *I saw the Holy City, the new Jerusalem, coming down out of heaven from God,*
> *prepared as a bride beautifully dressed for her husband.*
> *And I heard a loud voice from the throne saying,*
> *"Now the dwelling of God is with men,*
> *and he will live with them.*
> *They will be his people,*
> *and God himself will be with them*
> *and be their God.*
> *(Revelation 21:2, 3).*

The "new creation" of redeemed humanity will live with God in a "new city" that is wonderful beyond human description. It is beyond evil, beyond pain, beyond death, and beyond time. Oh, what a wonderful city it will be!

Who will inhabit God's city? Why was the eternal city created?

> *The city does not need the sun or the moon to shine on it,*
> *for the glory of God gives it light, and the Lamb is its lamp.*
> *The nations will walk by its light,*
> *and the kings of the earth will bring their splendor into it.*
> *The glory and honor of the nations will be brought into it.*
> *Nothing impure will ever enter it,*
> *nor will anyone who does what is shameful and deceitful,*
> *but only those whose names are written in the Lamb's book of life*
> *(Revelation 21:23, 24, 26).*

Notice that nothing impure or sinful is allowed into the city, but the nations are there! They have now been cleansed from their sin. The work of world redemption is seen in its completed form in this wonderful vision of John. The nations glorify God by walking in His light. The kings of the earth, now made holy, are granted splendor with which they now honor the Great King of all.

The nations will glorify God by walking in His light.

> *Then the angel showed me*
> **the river of the water of life, as clear as crystal,**
> *flowing from the throne of God and of the Lamb*
> *down the middle of the great street of the city.*
> *On each side of the river stood the tree of life,*
> *bearing twelve crops of fruit, yielding its fruit every month.*
> **And the leaves of the tree are for the healing of the nations.**
> *No longer will there be any curse*
> *(Revelation 22:1-3a; emphasis mine).*

Jesus promised the woman at the well a drink of living water. Here His promise to the woman, and to all the nations of the world, is permanently fulfilled. The "river of the water of life" flows freely in this city.

The tree of life, separated from mankind since the fall of Adam and Eve, is once again made available to us. The leaves of the tree are for healing — "the healing of the nations!"

> *The angel said to me,*
> *"These words are trustworthy and true.*
> *The Lord, the God of the spirits of the prophets,*
> *sent his angel to show his servants*
> *the things that must soon take place" (Revelation 22:6).*

Now the *Missio Dei* is complete. The nations, healed and filled with life, are walking in the light of the Lord. This is the vision of the future that compels us forward. This is the vision of the future that motivated Jesus to obey His Father. God is on a mission, and He is sharing that mission with us!

Prayer #10

O Sovereign Lord,
We are amazed by the mercy of Heaven's Plan.
Your right hand has worked salvation
for all the nations of the Earth!
Like the believers who sing in Revelation 15,
we also must break forth in worship
when our eyes catch a glimpse
of the glory of the King of the nations:
"Great and marvelous are Your deeds, Lord God Almighty.
Just and true are Your ways, King of the ages.
Who will not fear You, O Lord,
and bring glory to Your name?
For You alone are holy.
All nations will come
and worship before You,
for Your righteous acts
have been revealed."
(Revelation 15:3b-4)
Amen!

Figure 11.2

The Song of the Spirit and the Bride

Immediately after mankind fell into sin at the beginning of the Bible, we can hear God asking a question. His Spirit is grieved and His voice is filled with pain:

> *Then the man and his wife heard the sound of the Lord God*
> *as he was walking in the garden in the cool of the day,*
> *and they hid from the Lord God among the trees of the garden.*
> *But the Lord God called to the man,*
> *"Where are you?"*
> *(Genesis 3:8, 9).*

"Adam, where are you?" was the sad cry of the Creator. Mankind had fallen away from God and away from grace. The relationship between mankind and God had been broken. Through all of human history, no nation of men has ever been able to restore that relationship with God on its own.

However, God is loving and immensely rich in mercy. God devised a plan to help us. God has offered His free salvation to anyone who will believe on the saving work of Jesus Christ. The *Missio Dei* is the preaching of this gospel to every nation by the power of the Spirit.

Now as the Bible arrives at its completion, the Holy Spirit calls out to mankind again. The voices of angels and heavenly choirs grow still as a new song is raised. The song is God's heart cry for the nations of the earth! God has cried out to lost humanity, "Where are you?" Now a song is raised that invites a lost humanity to return to God!

The leading Singer is the blessed Holy Spirit of God. However, the voice of the Holy Spirit is now being joined by another. Hear the sound of the beautiful Bride of Christ — the redeemed people of God — joining in the Holy Spirit's song!

> *The Spirit and the bride say, "Come!"*
> *And let him who hears say, "Come!"*
> *Whoever is thirsty, let him come;*
> *and whoever wishes, let him take*
> *the free gift of the water of life*
> *(Revelation 22:17).*

Together, the Spirit and the Bride are making God's great mercy known. They are offering salvation to every human soul who is weary of sin. They are promising healing to everyone who is thirsty for water of life.

God is on a Mission, and He has given us a part in His great work. We can know Him, and we can represent Him to all nations. We can join in God's purposes for this earth. We can take our place as the Bride of Christ, His church. We can join with the Spirit as He sings His song to a lost and hopeless human race.

> *Together, the Spirit and the Bride are making God's great mercy known.*

Here is the purpose of the church. Here is God-given meaning and dignity for our lives. How could we ask for any greater gift? Hallelujah!

Responses

1. Take the time to sing a song of worship. If you are studying with others, please take some time to join in corporate prayer of commitment to participate in the Mission of God through the power of the Spirit. God will use this time to move on His people as you pray!

2. In the space below, write a prayer of your personal commitment to serve God by working in His Mission. Then share your prayer with a teacher, classmate, or friend.

My Prayer of Response to the Missio Dei

Figure 11.3

Summary

The book of Revelation describes the victorious completion of the *Missio Dei*. Those who take its message to heart will live differently and will one day be blessed. All of the covenants God made with His people have led up to the New Covenant in which God promised to live with us. John saw the fulfillment of these promises.

At last, Satan and evil are forever destroyed. Sinners saved by God's matchless grace are redeemed and brought, holy, into God's presence. The redeemed of every nation will live with God in the eternal city, and the water of life will flow and the leaves of the tree of life will be for the healing of the nations.

That day is coming soon. Until that day arrives, the Spirit and the Bride work together to call the nations to salvation. Whoever is thirsty may come, and God will dwell with them. The heaven for all nations is waiting!

Review and Application

Now that you have completed your study *The Biblical Theology of Missions,* you have learned that this theme runs systematically through the Word of God from Genesis to Revelation. The questions you must ask yourself are these: "What practical effect will my knowledge of *Missio Dei* have on my attitudes, values, and my work?" And, "How does the mission of God help me understand my call to ministry and service and my accountability to God for my stewardship?"

1. List three ways that a Christian could "take to heart" the message of the book of Revelation. Discuss your answers in the class.

2. Make a list of things that will be changed by the final victory of the Kingdom of God.

3. Why could the heaven of John's vision be best described as "A Heaven for All Nations?"

4. How would you feel if a neighbor from another nation moved in next door to your family?

5. Based on the previous question, do you think your heart is prepared for your new neighbors in heaven?

6. We are preparing the church for eternal life in heaven. Who must we try to bring with us to that city?

Be prepared to discuss these questions and any other questions or issues that come to mind when your instructor refers to them in class.

Glossary

The following list of words represents terms that have been defined in the context (chapter) where they first appeared. These words were used because they seemed to convey the meaning intended better than an alternate term. The number to the right of each term indicates the chapter where it was first used.

across time	— books that tell a story usually have a lesson or common theme that can be studied from beginning to end, *across time*	1
allocation	— practice of studying an unfinished task, dividing it, and assigning it to groups	4
Alpha and Omega	— the first and last letters of the Greek alphabet used in writing the New Testament	11
analysis	— a statement of conclusions reached by careful study and observation	6
anticipate	— to look forward with excitement for arrival of future event	8
apocalypse	— to uncover or unveil; a book of dramatic and symbolic prophecy, complete with terrible final judgments for some and glorious deliverance for others; the book of Revelation is sometimes known as *The Apocalypse*	11
apostle	— one who has been sent out on a mission; today, this word usually refers to one of the twelve original disciples of Christ who first planted the church in other cultures in and around the Roman Empire;	9

a) In this text, *primary apostle of Christ* refers to one of the original Twelve (plus Paul) sent out by Christ Himself to plant the first churches and establish sound doctrine

b) In this text, *secondary apostle* refers to many other men and women sent by the early church as church planters (often crossing cultures); today these official church representatives referred to as "missionaries"

charter	— founding document or constitution of a new organization, lays out the goals and commitments of a new working relationship	5
commission	— a strategic task assigned by a leader; delegated authority to someone to do a task as one's representative	8
common theme	— the idea or principle that runs throughout a written work and organizes it	1
covenant	— a promise agreement in which two parties willingly agree to requirements in order to form a lasting relationship	2
custody	— person kept under guard while waiting for trial	10
cynical	— attitude marked by a negative, depressed opinion on the purpose of life; cynic finds fault with the actions and intentions of other people	6
demography	— the science of studying the location and needs of human populations	4
disciple *(verb)*	— to *disciple* someone for Christ is to share life with that person as a mentor until that one understands Christ's character and calling and is successfully Following His way of life and ministry	9
discipling	— the process of making disciples referred to as *discipling* (Note: this term is <u>not</u> the same word as disciplining," which means the enforcement of correction, structure, or punishment.)	9
dynasty	— continuing line of kings	5
epistle	— scholarly name of an important letter that has been preserved for others to read	10
eternal	— what exists beyond time, not confined by a beginning or an end	1
ethnic group	— group of people that is distinct from other people in its language, race, and/or culture	
eunuch	— man made physically unable to have sexual relations so he could serve as a servant or official who worked in a queen's palace	9

evangelism demographics	— work that requires church leadership to survey the human populations around them and plan for their evangelization and discipleship	4
foretelling	— predicting what is going to happen in the future	7
Gentile	— any non-Jewish person; Jews in the New Testament believed Gentiles were excluded from God's covenant with Israel	3
gospel	— means "good news;" in Christian theology, the gospel is the good news that the death, resurrection, and rule of Jesus Christ brings salvation to everyone who believes in Him	8
grace	— special favor that is not deserved or earned by the one who receives it	2
heir	— one who inherits the possessions of another person, usually the person's child	3
hellenization	— refers to spread of Greek culture and language around the world during the time of the classical Greek Empire; *hellenization* derived from Hellas, another name for Greece; this broad cultural change was similar to the *westernization* of cultures happening in the contemporary world	8
inhabited	— place where people live; God is King of the entire inhabited earth; no human society is outside the scope of His kingdom	4
inheritance	— what one generation leaves for the next generation	4
kerygma	— the content of the message of the early apostles that focused on Jesus' death, resurrection, and on the need for the hearers to repent	9
kingdom	— ruling authority, effective power, an actual area belonging to a king (also called his *domain* or *dominion*)	4
kingdom of God	— part of creation that cooperates with the rule of God	4

kingdom of — refers to God's plan for His people to be a   3
kingdom of *priests* to stand between Himself
and people in order to bless all nations

lament — to mourn aloud, wail; song or poetry written   6
to mourn a great loss and to help people
remember what was lost

lawsuit — legal action brought before a judge in court;   7
a lawsuit accuses another party of breaking a
binding agreement or law; seeks to change the
other party's behavior

legacy — the lasting inheritance (or life lesson) left by   3
someone after he or she dies

lineage — list of a person's ancestors; one's family   5
lineage was important to know and remember
in Israelite culture during Bible days

manifest — to be evident, clear, and visible; God's *manifest*   4
presence is His clear, observable blessing on
His people

Messiah — the Anointed One, God's promised Servant and   7
Messenger, Who saves His people from their
sins

metaphor — figure of speech in which one word or phrase   6
is used to represent another because of an
implied similarity between the two; for
example, (Jeremiah 1:18)

meter — a literary device used in some poetry; each line   6
may be of the same length and the emphasis is
placed on the same syllables of each line

missio Dei — a Latin theological term meaning "mission of   1
God

mission — coordinated set of activities used to reach a   1
specific goal

mission of God — God's plan to advance His Kingdom throughout   1
the world through the preaching of the gospel

nations — ethnic and social groups of people, not political   3
kingdoms

normative	— the way things are always supposed to happen; if the process described in a story is normative, the account can be used for teaching or training purposes	9
omnipresent	— theological term meaning "present everywhere at the same time;" only God has this quality; since God is omnipresent, He is at work in every nation	
parallel	— two lines that run in the same direction without touching; parallel thoughts are thoughts stated in different ways that mean the same thing	6
Pentateuch	— first five books of the Bible called the *Pentateuch*	1
people group	— collection of people who feel that they share a common language and cultural identity	3
priest	— someone who stands between men and God in order to connect man and God in an ongoing covenant relationship	3
prophecy	— (noun) an authoritative message of the truth on behalf of God, spoken obediently under His direct anointing	7
prophesy	— (verb) to give an authoritative message from God to a person or group of people (the letter "s" in the verb replaces the letter "c" in the noun)	7
prophet	— someone who speaks a specific message from God by God's direct command	7
proverb	— a short, vivid statement that captures a practical truth in memorable words; proverbs often used to pass on wisdom in verbal societies	6
redeem	— to buy back	4
redemptive plan	— God's plan to redeem (buy back from sin) lost people from every nation on earth	10
rhyme	— device used in modern poetry and songs in which ending words of separate lines of poetry have the same sounds	6

Glossary

scope	— area of effective involvement or control	4
Shema	— statement that reveals God's nature which is found in Deuteronomy 6:4-5; the fact that there is only one God shows God's right to rule over all nations in a covenant relationship	3
situational epistle	— letter written in response to an actual event or "situation" in the life of the early church and its missionary outposts	10
surveyors	— those who measure and write down the precise boundaries and descriptions of land so it may be used legally	4
universal	— something found in every person or every place	6

Bibliography

Barker, Kenneth, ed. *The NIV Study Bible.* Grand Rapids: Zondervan, 1995.

Coleman, Robert. *The Master Plan of Evangelism.* Second Edition, Abridged. Grand Rapids: Baker Book House, 1993.

Gove, Philip, ed. *Webster's Third New International Dictionary of the English Language, Unabridged.* Springfield, MA: Merriam-Webster Inc., 2002.

Hesselgrave, David J. *Paradigms in Conflict: 10 Key Questions in Christian Missions Today.* Grand Rapids: Kregel, 2005.

_____. *Planting Churches Cross-Culturally.* Grand Rapids: Baker, 1980.

Johnstone, Patrick and Jason Mandryk. *Operation World: 21ˢᵗ Century Edition.* Waynesboro, GA: Paternoster USA, 2001.

Kaiser, Walter C. *Mission in the Old Testament: Israel as a Light to the Nations.* Grand Rapids: Baker, 2000.

Miller, Denzil R. *Empowered for Global Mission: A Missionary Look at the Book of Acts.* USA: Life Publishers International, 2005.

Stamps, Donald C., ed. *The Full Life Study Bible (NIV).* Grand Rapids: Zondervan, 1992.

York, John V. *Missions in the Age of the Spirit.* Springfield, MO: Logion, 2000.

Chapter I Review Exercises

Multiple-Choice Questions. Circle the letter preceding the correct answer.

1. God's mighty acts
   a) are designed to prove that He is God.
   b) are designed to punish sinners.
   c) are in agreement with His divine plan.
   d) will never be repeated.

2. God is on a mission
   a) that he alone will accomplish .
   b) and He is sharing that mission with us.
   c) that He is sharing with the Holy Spirit.
   d) and it will be revealed when Jesus returns.

3. *Missio Dei* refers to the
   a) Peace of God.
   b) Mission for Tomorrow.
   c) Mission of God.
   d) Mission Impossible.

4. Though the Bible contains history, poetry, prophecies, gospels, and letters it
   a) is actually one great story.
   b) contains many stories with unrelated themes.
   c) is very difficult to understand without many years of study.
   d) it should be studied with an open mind.

5. The fact that God was there before time began, and lives beyond time, unconfined by a beginning or an end, means that God is
   a) "pre-existent" and "eternal."
   b) "love" and 'all-forgiving."
   c) "all-powerful" and "all-knowing."
   d) "truth" and "worthy of praise."

6. Anyone made in the image of God
   a) will certainly become a Christian.
   b) lacks the capability of knowing God.
   c) can know God but cannot represent Him.
   d) is capable of knowing and representing God.

Chapter 2 Review Exercises

Multiple-Choice Questions. Circle the letter preceding the correct answer.

1. Our free choice to serve God is important because
   a) God wants us to serve Him willingly.
   b) we do NOT really have a choice in serving God.
   c) God created evil and uses it to bend our will.
   d) our will was created to help us be independent from God.

2. When Adam and Eve sinned, God could have destroyed them, but didn't because
   a) they were made in God's image and were valuable to Him.
   b) He was waiting to punish them severely.
   c) He couldn't since they had become like Him.
   d) He wanted to teach all mankind a lesson.

3. *He will crush your head, and you will strike his heel* is a promise that is called the
   a) Vengeance of God.   c) First Gospel.
   b) First Mistake.   d) Reason for Punishment.

4. Although the story of the flood shows that our sin causes God great pain, it also speaks of God's
   a) punishment for sin by wiping out mankind.
   b) grace by saving Noah.
   c) great anger by sending a flood to punish all mankind.
   d) guilt for sin by saving one family.

5. The Tower of Babel represents
   a) God's attempt to reach mankind.
   b) man's attempt to serve God.
   c) God's attempt to redeem the relationship with His creation.
   d) man's attempt create his own religion and way to heaven.

6. The Tower of Babel story answers: "Where did the nations come from?" and
   a) "Who are the nations that God will bless?"
   b) "Why did evil enter the world?"
   c) "How should God be worshipped?"
   d) "What kind of house should we build for God?"

Chapter 3 Review Exercises

Multiple-Choice Questions. Circle the letter preceding the correct answer.

1. The "Fiery Center" of the Word of God refers to
   a) God's punishment for sin by the creation of hell.
   b) Jesus' temptation in the desert for 40 days by Satan.
   c) God's covenant with Moses on the mountain covered with fire and smoke.
   d) God's covenant with Abraham, "all the peoples on earth will be blessed through you."

2. Abram's name was changed to Abraham to represent that he would be
   a) responsible to guard the promise that God gave him.
   b) known as the father of many nations.
   c) a small part of God's mission.
   d) tested severely before God gave him the fulfillment of God's covenant.

3. God counted Abram's trusting faith as righteousness because Abram
   a) had a special relationship with God.
   b) chose to believe God.
   c) helped God fulfill God's covenant.
   d) waited until the right moment to obey God.

4. When God "cut a covenant with Abraham," He
   a) promised Abraham He would make his offspring a blessing to all nations.
   b) promised Abraham that He would make Abraham very rich.
   c) made Abraham enter in the covenant by walking between the sacrifices.
   d) assured Abraham that the covenant would be fulfilled if he did not sin.

5. God made a covenant with Abraham to
   a) help God fulfill His promise to Abraham.
   b) make God's plans more certain to himself.
   c) let everyone know that the covenant was necessary.
   d) make Abraham more certain of His intentions.

Chapter 4 Review Exercises

Multiple-Choice Questions. Circle the letter preceding the correct answer.

1. To be complete, a kingdom must have three qualities: the
   a) right, the power, and the effectiveness to rule
   b) authority, the power, and the scope to rule.
   c) authority, the wisdom, and the power to rule.
   d) understanding, the time, and the scope to rule.

2. The book of Joshua tells us how
   a) the Israelites lost their kingdom and land.
   b) Joshua earned the right to lead the Israelites.
   c) Moses prepared the Israelites to become a kingdom to bless the nations.
   d) Israel received its land, and began to form the Kingdom that God intended.

3. One reason Israel was ordered to destroy the nations of Canaan was that
   a) only Israelites could be the kingdom of priests destined to bless the nations.
   b) the occupants of Canaan weren't ready to be blessed by God as Israel was.
   c) the Amorites extremely wicked and would not change their evil ways.
   d) God's plans didn't include other nations; His blessing was just for Israelites.

4. In Joshua chapter 1, Joshua learned that the first step in obeying God was to
   a) remember God's word.
   b) destroy the evil nations.
   c) lead the nation of Israel.
   d) make no decisions checking with the priests.

5. The process of public accountability to finish a task is called
   a) delegation.
   b) allocation.
   c) leadership.
   d) demographics.

Chapter 5 Review Exercises

Multiple-Choice Questions. Circle the letter preceding the correct answer.

1. A biblical leader whose leadership plan was similar to that of Jesus was
   a) Moses.   b) Joshua.   c) Samuel.   d) David.

2. The book of Ruth portrays the theology of the *Missio Dei* because Ruth
   a) obeyed her mother-in-law when she moved back to Israel.
   b) married into a powerful family and became an ancestor to King David.
   c) was a girl from another nation who was included in Kingdom blessings.
   d) established her place in history by doing what her sister-in-law wouldn't do.

3. God's declaration in the book of Ruth is that
   a) anyone who seeks God may become part of God's covenant people.
   b) people with a sinful past may be included in God's covenant people.
   c) it is difficult to overcome one's past and be part of God's covenant people.
   d) men are more acceptable than women in the covenant people of God.

4. The Covenant of the Kingdom in 2 Samuel 7 was established between God and
   a) Saul.   b) Samuel   c) David   d) Solomon

5. Although David was not allowed to build God's house, God promised him:
   a) "Your house and your kingdom will endure forever."
   b) "You will be a man of war for all of your life."
   c) "Your children will go into captivity."
   d) "You will go to your grave in peace."

6. David's eternal covenant is fulfilled by the ministry of
   a) Solomon.   b) Israel.   c) Paul.   d) Jesus.

Chapter 6 Review Questions

Multiple-Choice Questions. Circle the letter preceding the correct answer.

1. Because the book of Job was probably written before other books of the Bible and doesn't mention the Law of Moses, it can show us that God
   a) cares primarily for the nation of Israel.
   b) did not inspire the message of this book.
   c) shows how His wisdom is superior to man's wisdom.
   d) shows how He cares for people of all nations.

2. We identify over 40 *Missio Dei* Psalms in Psalms since they deal with the
   a) salvation of the nations.   c) nation of Israel.
   b) punishment of the sinful.   d) end of the age.

3. The 47th Psalm shows the connection between the covenants with
   a) Moses and Jesus.   c) Joshua and David.
   b) Abraham and David.   d) Job and Jesus.

4. According to the 67th Psalm the purpose of God's blessings is that we
   a) know that God loves us with an everlasting love.
   b) can show that our God is the King of the universe.
   c) may reflect the light of His salvation to the nations.
   d) will follow God all the days of our life.

5. The story of the Queen of Sheba's visit to King Solomon proved that Israel
   a) was superior to all the surrounding nations.
   b) served its purpose as a kingdom of priests for the nation of Sheba.
   c) wouldn't be able to fulfill its purpose as a kingdom of priests because of sin.
   d) would endure forever because of its special covenant.

6. The wisdom of God's kingdom in Proverbs/Wisdom Literature shows that
   a) the nations could see the wisdom of Israel.
   b) Israel could better show that only David would be the eternal King.
   c) Israel could communicate truth about God to other nations.
   d) the nations the folly of trying to defeat the nation of Israel.

Chapter 7 Review Exercises

Multiple-Choice Questions. Circle the letter preceding the correct answer.

1. Those who served the *Missio Dei* by working as God's "Covenant "enforcement agents" were the
   a) Priests.   b) Kings.   c) Psalmists.   d) Prophets.

2. The prophets say the nations will receive salvation, discipleship, and will
   a) never completely submit to God's authority.
   b) never be equal with the nation of Israel.
   c) worship the one who is worthy – King Jesus.
   d) only submit to Jesus' rule after the millennial reign.

3. According to Isaiah, the Messiah would
   a) come as a humble servant.
   b) come in power and authority.
   c) be accepted by His own people.
   d) conquer the armies of Rome.

4. The restoration of David's fallen tent in the book of Amos meant that
   a) the physical reign of the descendants of David would be restored.
   b) God would discard the nation of Israel and begin with a new people.
   c) God had not forgotten David's Kingdom or His *charter for the nations.*
   d) God was about to destroy the nations who had attacked Israel.

5. The day of Pentecost brought fulfillment to the prophecy by the prophet
   a) Jeremiah.   b) Isaiah.   c) Joel.   d) Amos.

6. Jonah has a unique place in the development of the *Missio Dei* because
   a) God called him, a Jew, to preach repentance to a Gentile city.
   b) Jonah went willingly to preach to the foreign city of Nineveh.
   c) Jonah preached God's gospel of salvation to the lost citizens of Nineveh.
   d) God judged Jonah, even though he was a Jew.

Chapter 8 Review Exercises

Multiple-Choice Questions. Circle the letter preceding the correct answer.

1. Which of the following titles for the Savior from the Matthew's genealogy refers to the blessing for all nations?
   a) Jesus Christ
   b) Son of Abraham
   c) Son of David
   d) Son of God

2. A key purpose of parables is to cause hearers to think about the twin themes of the
   a) Power and the Glory.
   b) Kingdom and the Nations.
   c) Teachings and the Sermons.
   d) Praise and the Worship.

3. The eleventh hour laborers are involved in
   a) the task of protecting the church from association with lost sinners.
   b) resisting the attacks of Satan until they are rescued by the rapture.
   c) the crucial decisions about who to elect or choose to rule over the churches.
   d) the last moments of the harvest of the souls of mankind.

4. The Greek word the Gospel of John uses that shows us God's ongoing commit ment to the *Missio Dei* is
   a) *kurios* (Lord).
   b) *theos* (God).
   c) *kosmos* (the earth).
   d) *anthropos* (man).

5. John gives us a valuable insight into Jesus' own sense of His mission in John 10 when He said
   a) "I have other sheep that are not of this sheep pen. I must bring them also."
   b) "Blessed are those who mourn, for they shall be comforted."
   c) "I say to you, love your enemies and pray for those who persecute you."
   d) "When you give to the poor, do not let your left hand know what your right hand is doing."

6. The greatest single job that God has ever delegated to mankind was the
   a) Great Commission.
   b) Lord's Prayer.
   c) Day of Pentecost.
   d) Teachings of Jesus.

Chapter 9 Review Exercises

Multiple-Choice Questions. Circle the letter preceding the correct answer.

1. A better name of the book of Acts might be the Acts of the
   a) Apostles.
   b) Holy Spirit Working in believers.
   c) Risen Lord through His church.
   d) Followers of Jesus Christ.

2. The believer's main source of power to advance *Missio Dei* to the ends of the earth would come from the
   a) process of classroom learning.
   b) prayers of believers.
   c) baptism of the Holy Spirit.
   d) worship of God the Father.

3. The essential points of the gospel are called the
   a) *Koinonia.*   b) *Gnosis.*   c) *Kerygma.*   d) *Glossolalia.*

4. Without Christ's gift of the Holy Spirit, we may do some good at times,
   a) but we will probably not be able to tell the difference.
   b) but we will never complete the Christ's commission.
   c) and we will see many miracles.
   d) and we will be able to accomplish the Great Commission.

5. The first Christian who devoted himself full-time to International Discipleship was
   a) Barnabas.   b) Paul.   c) Peter.   d) Stephen.

6. When Paul and Barnabas finished the missionary cycle and returned to Antioch, they showed an important missionary principle: the missionary is
   a) accountable for his or her ministry to the local church.
   b) responsible to his or her organization to evangelize every people group.
   c) required to make discipleship of new believers his or her highest priority.
   d) d) limited by the conditions on his or her field for any success in ministry.

7. The first European church was founded in the city of
   a) Antioch.   b) Rome.   c) Athens.   d) Philippi.

Chapter 10 Review Exercises

Multiple-Choice Questions. Circle the letter preceding the correct answer.

1. Paul's letters can be best understood as
   a) discipleship guides for the church to follow.
   b) amazing stories of the acts of Jesus.
   c) lists of complaints and corrections.
   d) new strategies that would change the nature of the church.

2. The effective force behind Paul's ministry to the Gentiles was
   a) the quality of his hard work and planning.
   b) Paul's status as an apostle.
   c) the demonstrated power of the Holy Spirit.
   d) his education as a Pharisee.

3. Paul did not evangelize Troas because
   a) Troas was not open to the gospel.
   b) Paul did not have a long-term worker ready to be the pastor.
   c) Paul did not think that Troas was ready for a church.
   d) Troas was bound by the power of Satan.

4. Paul's missionary discipleship strategy involved what four groups of people?
   a) Leaders, Workers, Disciples, and the Lost.
   b) Apostles, Prophets, Priests, and Disciples.
   c) Leaders, Pastors, Teachers, and Disciples.
   d) Workers, Learners, Leaders, and Disciples.

5. Paul tells the Galatians that the unchanging faith in God's plan to save all nations was known as the
   a) Covenant of David.
   b) Gospel of Abraham.
   c) Gospel of the Kingdom.
   d) Good News for all people.

6. The story of the expansion of the church in the New Testament
   a) had a clear ending with the death of the apostles.
   b) continued until the early church was established.
   c) had no clear ending, and we are living out the story of *Missio Dei*.
   d) is slowly coming to an end.

Chapter 11 Review Exercises

Multiple-Choice Questions. Circle the letter preceding the correct answer.

1. God has dealt with mankind from the very beginning by using
   a) His power to destroy sin.
   b) the promises of His covenants.
   c) the revelation of the prophets.
   d) the preaching of the apostles.

2. The book of Revelation reveals judgment on Satan specifically because he
   a) deceived the nations of the earth.
   b) refused to ask forgiveness from God d) lied to Adam and Eve.
   c) had a faulty line of ancestors.

3. The thing that will make heaven great — beyond comparison — is the
   a) absence of sin.   c) fulfillment of His covenant.
   b) perfection of our bodies. d) presence of God.

4. The praise of the elders in heaven reveals that Christ suffered to
   a) punish the nations.   c) bless all nations.
   b) prove that He is the Son of God. d) save His own life.

5. The purpose of the leaves of the tree of life is
   a) the healing of the nations.
   b) to provide shade for the followers of Jesus.
   c) a mystery that is not revealed.
   d) the Good News for all people.

6. The answer to the to the Creator's sad cry, "Adam where are you?" is answered at the end of the *Missio Dei* by the song of
   a) Christ, "It is finished!"
   b) angels, "Worthy is the Lamb!"
   c) earth's new dwellers, "We will worship."
   d) the Spirit and the Bride, "Come!"

Printed in the Republic of Belarus
Minsk Colour Printing Factory.
20, Korzhenevsky Str., Minsk, 220024.